The Thai and I

The Thai and I
Thai Culture and Society

Roger Welty

ASIA BOOKS

Published and Distributed by
Asia Books Co.,Ltd
No# 65/66, 65/70, 7th Floor,
Chamnan Phenjati Business Center
Rama 9 Road, Huaykwang
Bangkok 10320 Thailand
Tel: (66 2) 715-9000
Fax: (66 2) 715-9197
E-mail: information@asiabooks.com
www.asiabooks.com

First published 1996 by Community Services Association of Bangkok.
Second Edition published 2004 by Asia Books Co., Ltd.

 Illustrations by Prawit Mongkolnawarat.

Typeset by COMSET Limited Partnership.
Printed in Thailand.

ISBN 978-974-8303-96-3

Contents

The Thai and I:
Understanding Your Hosts

What About. . . ?
Time, Titles, Toilets, and Other Tidbits

A Note About This Edition

We all hope to be remembered after we pass through this world, or even better yet, that something we created lingers long through time. Roger Welty has achieved that through a wonderful book he wrote in the mid-1990s.

Mr. Welty died in Bangkok in July 2003. And the Community Services of Bangkok, for which he worked and which commissioned and published his book, closed down a year earlier. But with Asia Books acquiring the copyright to *The Thai and I* from CSB, Mr. Welty's presence in Thailand and cultural insights live on. Though Mr. Welty's original version, published in 1996, was a hefty single volume, this second edition has been divided in half to produce two easier-to-carry editions. Mr. Welty's light-hearted voice and first-person storytelling remain as they originally appeared, when he was still alive. It may seem odd at times, especially when he writes of hoping to die in Bangkok, but to change his voice would have been to create a completely different book.

In addition, the foreword has remained largely the same, and because of the valuable contribution of various people in the first publication, their names are listed in the acknowledgements.

Mr. Welty brought to this book three decades of understandings and misunderstandings and all-around experiences. It is intended to help newcomers adjust to living in Thailand more easily, and to find the splendour of the country and its people, as Mr. Welty gloriously did.

Foreword

They say we are all outsiders when we travel. And I would add that not only when we travel, but when we decide to go and live abroad we can forever be complete outsiders unless. . . .

This book is meant to fill in that blank and spell out the unspoken. *The Thai and I: Thai Culture and Society* is aimed at helping transform its readers from 'outsiders' into 'insiders.' It helps expats learn to feel at home in Thailand, at ease with Thais, and at peace with themselves amidst unfamiliar surroundings.

From time immemorial, either sheer wanderlust or economic necessity has taken people many miles from their native lands, either for temporary sojourn or permanent settlement. Migration is indeed as old as humanity itself, and is integral to human development. Chinese travellers were frequently seen charting, exploring, and, of course, trading around the vast expanse of Asian waters as far back as two millennia ago. In more recent times (dating from the Age of Discovery in the fifteenth century) Europeans, in particular, ventured far and wide to the four corners of the globe. They generated an unprecedented, massive transplantation of human resources. This was not only in the form of traders or settlers, but of such types as Kipling's proverbial 'white man,' engaged in the 'pre-destined task' of enlightening the 'darker regions' of the earth. To Thailand (or Siam, as it was then known) and other countries of the East, the white man also came. But, unlike in most of those other countries, he came to Thailand without ever assuming the 'burden' of civilizing through govern-ance. Foreigners, especially Westerners, living and working on Siamese soil, have been aplenty through the ages. But whatever profession they followed, none of them ever was a pro-consul from a 'mother' country.

Ever since the mid-nineteenth century, it has been the consistent policy of Siamese and Thai rulers to open up the country and maintain friendly relations with the Western world. In fact, Thailand intentionally turned to the outside world as the source of knowledge and technology in the process of modernizing the ancient kingdom. Without the constraint of having to rely on a single colonial authority, Siam could thus exercise freedom of choice and association in seeking and obtaining the best knowledge from virtually every Western country. Foreign experts have helped and continue to assist in various aspects of overall national development.

And so it came to pass about a hundred years ago that the then king's chief advisor (a position comparable to the modern-day prime minister) was a distinguished Belgian jurist, while the first commander-in-chief of the modern Royal Thai Navy was a Dane of French-Huguenot origin. Yet another Dane served as a chief of police. This same position was also occupied at another time by a British Channel Islander. After the First World War, when Siam's efforts were focused on extricating herself from the unequal treaties earlier imposed by major European powers, American expertise in the field of international law was much relied upon. This was shown particularly well by the dedicated service of the eminent Francis B. Sayre. A Bangkok street (running alongside the Foreign Ministry) has been named after him, using his Thai title of Phya Kalyana Maitri. All the while, the country continued to benefit from the good work carried out by a vast array of industrious expatriates, ranging from French missionary school teachers, British railway engineers, to German doctors and Italian architects.

Diverse indeed were these sources of foreign contribution to the country's progress. But more significantly, such co-operative endeavours helped to generate a lasting sense of trust, friendship, and affection. A large reservoir of goodwill was created, and has existed since those days, marking Thailand as an old and trusted friend, ever ready to extend a hearty welcome to all. Such natural warmth and spontaneity from the host should make life a little easier for the newly arrived guest. It is up to him or her to build on this solid rock.

The diversity of foreign contacts that Thailand has enjoyed matches well with its intrinsically diverse ethnic and cultural background and heritage. Thailand is at the crossroads of Southeast Asia, not only in the geographical but also the cultural sense. We are at the confluence of two important streams of world civilization, with the Sino-Confucian to the east and the Indo-Mon-Khmer to the west. Indo-Chinese traits are apparent in all manners and forms of our living. We have managed to synthesize and refine them into our own distinct identity. We are, in a manner of speaking, truly the people who not only eat noodles *and* curry, but also noodles *in* curry! And when it comes to our immediate neighbours to the north and south, again we are at a meeting point, with the Buddhist mainland to the north and the Muslim archipelagos to the south. Through the centuries, these crossroads have witnessed the coming of people from neighbouring lands. They stay and live here, mingling and becoming one with us. All this has helped to make Thailand a melting pot of a society, blessed by the prevalent Buddhist tenet of tolerance and the unifying force of the benevolent monarchy, thus engendering harmony amidst the many diverse constituent elements.

But Thailand basically is a traditional society. Ideally she will remain so—with a proven track record of her ability to adapt and adjust to changing times and circumstances. Indeed, customs, practices, and mores abound, which are expected to be strictly observed by one and all without any national or international distinction. It is noteworthy that this book, like others with similar aims, will offer words of advice to resident expatriates. Sometimes this advice is conveniently divided into do's and don'ts, all because of the obvious recognition of the cultural divide facing our overseas guests, particularly first-time visitors. The 'don'ts' may sound like old taboos that, in a rough, rigid, and ritualistic society would spell out untold dire consequences. However, in an open and more tolerant society like Thailand, less exacting demands are made of our welcomed friends from overseas. The 'do's' especially are left to the good judgement of our foreign guests. With keen, observant eyes and a bit of common sense, expats will never fail to please their hosts and add a feather to their cap by doing one of the 'do's' unexpectedly. Take, for example, the *wai*—that mark of respect, greeting, or recognition performed by bringing open palms together and synchronizing with a dip of the head or a bow (low, lower, or lowest, depending upon the level of veneration to be shown toward the person or object being addressed). The *wai* can be reckoned as the most subtle use and versatile form of body language. It can even be a cure-all or a saving grace when offered, especially rather unexpectedly by a foreigner when caught in an embarrassing situation or a social faux pas.

Cultural differences have given rise in the past to knotty problems of adjustment for expatriates. But in this new age of globalization, with its uniform, 'internationalized' way of living, it has been questioned whether the differences are still relevant. Are they not supposed to be buried in the global village characterized by brand-names and fast-food chains, 7-Eleven convenience stores, billboards advertising monotonously multinational soft drinks, or the ubiquitous karaoke lounges, be they in Bangkok, Jakarta, Dallas, or Amsterdam?

While such outward, physical sameness may help to make a foreign housewife shopping in a Bangkok mall feel as if she is back home at Tysons Corner in Fairfax County, USA, let her beware lest she should be misled by the all too apparent and even deceptive similarities. While the global burger chains will contend that their burger is deliciously the same wherever eaten, there is still merit in the counter-contention that it can never taste the same in Bangkok as in Bloomington! For that, thanks may be attributed to the presentation or even the milieu! There will always be those who will shout '*Vive la difference*!'

Living abroad is an enriching experience, particularly when viewed with the benefit of hindsight. But it can become a trying time if one refuses to make necessary adjustments. From my own experience of living and working overseas for the better part of my thirty-year diplomatic career, I have no doubt that whatever station in life one finds oneself in when abroad (including even leading the so-called charmed life of a diplomat), in the final analysis one simply has to learn to relate to the total surroundings if one wants really to 'live.'

As the title suggests, this book sets its sights high for a successful life in Thailand. But how does one define or even measure success in this context? A ready yardstick would be to gauge one's feeling in terms of time. If you feel that time has flown since your arrival, or that your two-year stay has seemed like just four months, then your life in Thailand must be considered a success! However, on closer scrutiny, you may discover that those imaginary four months aptly correspond to the time you spent cooped up in your car in the jam-packed streets of Bangkok. Horror of horrors! Alas, that is part of the reality of Bangkok life these days.

What better way to distract yourself from the pressures of life in Bangkok than to do some reading? And what better book than *The Thai and I*. If you live outside of Bangkok in this beautiful country, read it with the mood of relief that will come, with a renewed appreciation of wherever you are living in Thailand!

Ambassador Vitthya Vejjajiva,
Honorary Chairman, CSB,
January 1996.

The Late Roger Welty

"By accident of birth, Northern Californian. By choice, Southeast Asian," is the usual way Roger Welty referred to himself. Arriving in Thailand in the 1960s, Welty liked to say he had walked here, which was a neat trick if you consider some of the distance was over water.

Of a polyglot and mongrel background—Swiss-Mennonites, Bavarian draft-dodgers, runaway Huguenots, defeated Scots, Confederate refugees—whose family history parallels the immigrant waves to North America, Roger was raised in the Bay Area of San Francisco and in Mexico.

Even before the bridge was built, his dream was to sail out of the Golden Gate aboard one of the great ships he admired as a child when he visited San Francisco. On these jaunts, he had used his allowance to buy streetcar tokens and pay the ferry fare, and then ride cable cars and trams all day, exploring that compact but great city.

The best way was to stroll along the Embarcadero, not as it is now, all fancy restaurants and boutiques, but a real operating port with ships from all over the world. He ached to sail aboard one. His wish came true just as he graduated from the University of California in Asia-Economics, an 'individual group major,' the only recipient of this degree.

He sailed out under the Golden Gate as a third-class junior assistant purser (temp.) aboard the American President Lines' *President Wilson* in the first of several passages he was to make to Asia. He was prepared by his studies to try to cope with Arabic, Chinese *kuo yu*, and Siamese. The first he withdrew from, the second he failed, and the third, re-named Thai, he liked.

Admitted to university in Peking (Beijing), he couldn't go because of the communists. So after serving in the Korean War and a stint in Europe where he taught English and translated Ellery Queen murder mysteries into Spanish, he left once again for the East. Sailing from Barcelona on a Turkish ship, he proceeded by thumb, pushbike, train, truck, foot, and boat to India. He then travelled by sea to Malaysia and on again by foot and thumb to Bangkok, Cambodia, and Laos, and back to the Thai capital, where he settled.

This little outing took a year and eight months and cost 880 US dollars all told, including time in a Nepalese hospital. While there he wrote a novel, which he paid a Chinese dustman to cart away. "I'd have spent the rest of my life on that 1,000-page book." And so he took another writer's advice: "Toss out your first and then start for real." Real or not, the first volume of *The Thai and I* was the result of thirty years of living in Thailand, lecturing at two Thai universities teaching Thai, Buddhism, and *La Historia de Espana* in Castellano. He premiered two plays and also wrote a couple of hundred articles for papers and magazines in the region.

Liking to travel, he founded Eastern Horizons to explore Thailand with people who enjoyed going by boat, van, bus, truck, train—but not air. "Going by plane is the most expensive way to experience the least," Welty said.

Married and then unmarried, he adopted three Thai teenagers and "Wallowed in the *pater familias* role," becoming a grandfather in the 1990s.

From actor and playwright in California and New York, to ship's purser and guide on the Pacific, and Buddhist monk and high-school teacher in Thailand, Welty came to write his version of *The Thai and I* for CSB: "I could see the need the foreign population had here for a friend. The fine people at CSB provided a place for newcomers and oldcomers alike to meet, to study things Thai and Asian, and to learn about themselves. I wholeheartedly support this necessary work and was honoured when they invited me to become the principal author of *The Thai and I*," Welty wrote for the first edition.

And he signed off in that edition, "I hope you enjoy reading it as much as I have enjoyed writing it."

Acknowledgements

The original team for the first publication of *The Thai and I:*

Judy Kocher (CSB's executive director), David Bailey (CSB's counselling director), Toby Kambhu, Natalie Stewart, Suzanne Deas, Gro Christiansen, Amy Kaplan, Jonathan Harger, Julian Spindler, Dan Boyd, Ellen Lochaya, Steve Rosse, Dr. Esther Wakeman, Vasit Kasemsap, Manoon Phatraban, Phitsanu and Vaija Chandrakunphong, Saichon Prakobchai, Bancha Klomklio, Achaan Dr. Udom Warotamasikkhadit, Achaan Malithat Promathattavedi, Achaan Martin Schalbruch, Achaan Bradley Arnold, Ruth Gerson, John and Jan Blank, Sandra Moore, Dr. Irene Kiatkuankoon, Dr. Domenica Garcia, Achaan Nabhachari Nakvajara, Supramote Changwong, Achaan Mattani Mojdara Rutinin, and Christine Plaud.

"khrai khaai khai kai"

Author's Note on Spelling and Romanization

It has long been the custom for books on South and Southeast Asia to follow British spelling. Most newspapers and periodicals in what were British protectorates and colonies, of course, do this, and those in Thailand do, as well. Discussion amongst members of the CSB Book Committee (in 1995) determined that British spelling would be followed, although the grammar and personal writing style is American.

As for the Romanization from Thai into the English alphabet, there is a problem that is seemingly impossible of satisfactory solution. In former times, up to the end of the nineteenth century, European writers wrote what they thought they had heard—*Poottah* for 'Buddha,' *Nacorn* for 'Nakhon,' and so on. They also used a system developed to transliterate Indian languages, such as Sanskrit, Pali, Hindi, or Urdu. On a letter-by-letter basis, with a few variations, this works for Thai, as well.

It is no real problem changing Indic written consonants into Thai; the trouble lies in the vowels, and to use Indic vowels with the Indic consonants produces an Indian language, not Thai. If every educated Thai had studied Sanskrit or Pali, as they used to, there would be no problem. The same holds with English: if every English-writing person had studied his Latin or his Greek, he'd be much better at spelling English. Words with 'ise' or 'ize' endings, for example, would become clear.

Like English with its Greco-Latin ancestry, so is Thai with its Sanskrit and Pali history. Fortunately for Thais, those Indian languages were very closely related. Pali is a simplification of Sanskrit and, for the most part, uses the same alphabet as the Thais do.

The problems arise when a writer wishes to render words from the Thai alphabet into the English alphabet. For this there are three systems: Indic, also credited to King Rama VI; *Rajabandhityasathaan*, credited to the Royal Institute (with the spellings *Rajabandhit*, *Rajapandita*, *Ratchabandit*); and 'do-it-yourself' (DIY), the most common and also the most deforming, so that non-English readers are left in the dark. This last method is the one most commonly seen in the *Bangkok Post*, *The Nation*, and any other publication that uses Thai terms in a European language.

There are workable systems for Arabic, Russian, various Indian dialects, Inuit, Nahuatl, Xhosa, Navajo, and just about any language except Thai. Even Chinese has two workable systems.

In *The Thai and I*, we are not attempting to set up yet another system for Romanizing Thai for the convenience of expats. We occasionally employ two systems, the second only to indicate pronunciation of words in the other.

An example would be the Thai for 'lover' or 'sweetheart,' which in King Rama VI's Indic system would come out *di rak*; in the Royal Institute's form would be *thi rak*; and in the do-whatever-you-want manner, it might come out *tee ruck* or *tilac* or *tee rak*. Throughout this book we have endeavoured to show either Indic or DIY. This last will be based primarily on American pronunciations, such as *baan* instead of the British 'barn,' for 'village' or 'house.'

We hope by operating as we have to achieve two results. The first is faithfulness to the manner in which Thais themselves have attempted to deal with the problem. The second is to help non-Thais see in print what they see on signs and such, and to see what they hear, as well.

Roger Welty,
1995.

From Ancient Saddle Sores to Today's Traffic Jams: Old Siam and Modern Thailand

A Ride Through Thai History

There appears to be a historical mystery about the true origins of the Thai people. That they are an ancient race is well established. That they were once located to the north of present-day Thailand, somewhere in what is now Southwestern China, is hinted at by the existence today in Yunnan of Thai-speaking minorities. Of course, their Thai (or, as it is Romanized for them, Dai or T'ai) is not the same as today's Bangkok speech.

But there is another theory that the ethnic Thai originated in what are now Mongolia and Eastern Tibet, and were pushed south by the Han, the ancestors of today's Chinese. The Thai and Han peoples competed for space and resources. The Han were better organized and eventually more numerous, so they slowly drove the Thai southward into what is now Northern Thailand.

3

The proof offered by some Thais for a Mongolian origin is that Thai babies are born with a bruise-like mark on their bottoms. This mark, according to Mom Rajavong Seni Pramoj (a former prime minister and strong traditionalist), is a result of their ancestors' having ridden bareback across the steppes of Asia centuries ago.

I might add that Western-oriented scientists fail to accept this as proof of Mongolian origin; the bruise mark is found on other Asian babies' bottoms, too. Whatever may cause it, this genetic mark on Thai babies fades as they enter childhood and is usually gone by adolescence. Still, popular belief accepts this as proof of true Thainess.

About the beginning of the tenth century AD, these migrating Thais established a kingdom called Nan Chao, and then other kingdoms with different names as they drifted southward into the outer marches of the Khmer Empire. This empire, centred on Cambodia, was in decay. It was vastly over-extended, and as the Thais moved in to settle the border areas, they accepted a very light-handed Khmer rule. Thai tribes founded their own principalities under nominal Khmer control.

Eventually two Thai princes and their followers took advantage of the Khmers' weakness, rising in rebellion against the Khmer governor in Phitsanulok. One of these 'liberated' areas was Sukhodaya—Sukhothai,

as it became known later. Today it is the seat of a smallish province by the same name.

The immediate cause of this rebellion was water. It was not today's familiar struggle between two groups over water rights and usage. This was Water of Fealty, specially blessed water that vassals had to carry in large clay containers on carts all the way to the Khmer capital, where vassal princes would drink it as a declaration of their loyalty to the king.

The two Thai princes improved on the procedure by carrying their water not in clay jars (which often cracked on the rough journey) but by storing it in woven baskets made leak-proof with resin. As things turned out, the Khmer king was not at all pleased at this show of enterprise in his vassals. Perhaps he saw it as dangerously independent thinking. So he issued a secret command to his governor to seize and kill the Thai princes upon their return to the north. They got wind of this bit of regal treachery. Instead of allowing themselves to be captured and killed, they led a revolt that, in the end, freed their areas from the Khmers. A new Thai kingdom was set up and flourished.

This was all in the thirteenth century AD, about the time of the Crusades in Europe and the Near East. Independent Sukhothai expanded rapidly. Its third king, Ramkhamhaeng, is credited with all sorts of public improvements and the 'invention' of the Thai alphabet.

This last is probably not quite true. King Ramkhamhaeng (now called 'the Great') actually presided over a revision of the Khmer alphabet to better fit the Thai language. This king is regarded as one of early Thailand's greatest monarchs, and his rule spread over wide areas. Some historians say Sukhodayan rule extended southward as far as Singapore.

But nothing is unchanging in the world, especially in politics. In 1350 a prince from the west of Siam, U Thong, established a new kingdom based on an island defined by the convergence of major rivers of the central part of the country. On the north and west sides, the boundary was the Chao Phraya (which extends southward to Bangkok and the Gulf of Thailand). The Lopburi and Pa Sak rivers form the northern and eastern boundaries of the island, named after an important town in classical India—Ayodhya, or, in Thai, Ayuddhaya (with many variations in spelling, and now commonly spelled Ayutthaya).

From this excellent defensive position, Ayuddhaya rapidly became a military force. It absorbed Sukhothai and its dependent lands, also conquering Chiang Mai to the north, much of modern-day Laos, and the Khmer heartland to the east. Some areas to the west, now in Burma, were also taken by the Ayuddhayans, whose rule reached south to the middle of Malaya, as well.

Ayuddhayan forces invaded and looted the Khmer capital at Angkor Thom (the 'Great City'), forcing the Khmers to abandon it and move farther eastward to seek safety. In only a few more years, the tables completely turned: the Khmer kings became vassals of Ayuddhaya, and Cambodia remained a subject state until the French squeezed it from Siamese hands to take it into their own.

For 417 years—nearly twice as long as the United States has existed—Ayuddhaya reigned supreme. Its island position was reinforced by a great encircling wall, and it became the centre for traders from Arabia, Persia, India, Malaya, Java, and from China and Japan. From the 1500s onward, the Portuguese sought trading relations with the Ayuddhayan court. The Dutch followed, and then the English, all of whom received the king's permission to establish warehouses and sales offices of their own.

Ayuddhaya waxed rich on the trade that was 'taxed' by the king's officers who exercised the Crown's right to buy from the foreigners, to sell to his own subjects, and to buy from those same subjects such products as the Europeans wanted. The king and his officials were effectively middlemen in both directions.

One of the most fascinating stories of this period tells of a Cephalonian Greek who joined the English East India Company and within a very few years had left them to take over the king's office of '*barcalon,*' as it is called in old manuscripts. In effect he was the lord of the exchequer and the de facto foreign minister, running the king's business, which included dealing with foreign traders and putting the heaviest squeeze on them that he could get away with.

This talented and daring Greek, Constantine Phaulkon (or 'Falcon'), is famous in Siamese history for his devoted service to King Narai, who ennobled him. Phaulkon helped the king in his foreign relations, particularly with France. As was customary in the seventeenth century, he was not averse to lining his pockets with foreign gold and silver. He was able thus to put on a personal display that annoyed his former English employers enormously. In the 1680s, Phaulkon encouraged King Narai to enter into a correspondence with King Louis XIV of France, Europe's most powerful monarch at the time. Phaulkon did his best to convince Louis' missions

that King Narai was interested in the Christian religion, and also—but only incidentally, of course—in cannons and guns, and soldiers who could sail out to teach the Siamese how to make and use them.

Louis, modestly called the 'Sun King' at home, was most interested in expanding the Catholic Church's influence. He also wasn't called the 'Most Christian King' for nothing. There were advantages to France in encouraging the spread of French Catholicism into the Far East. For one thing, along with Spain in the Philippines, it would help counter the Protestant Dutch and English interests in the region.

Thus, Louis had no objection to providing a bishop or two for the religious instruction of King Narai. In his embassy to Siam, he even included a small detachment of soldiers and some armourers and cannon smiths as requested. But these last were not so important from the Sun King's point of view, although that may seem unbelievably naïve today.

Constantine Phaulkon won King Narai's confidence entirely and, over time, managed to exaggerate to the French the Siamese king's interest in their religion, even dangling before them the prospect of his possible conversion to Catholicism. Phaulkon played a double game, noticed certainly by envious Ayuddhaya courtiers, to mis-inform both kings of the true intentions and desires of the other. The purpose of this was to seek trade advantages for Siam and thus for himself. In these tangled affairs, Phaulkon cleverly played the French, Dutch, and English against each other. Since that time, the Thais have become practiced experts at this form of politics, much to their own benefit.

One result of all this was that King Narai sent embassies to Europe (one was lost at sea off Southern Africa) and King Louis responded by sending his representatives to Ayuddhaya. The plot thickened when Phra Phetraja, an important Siamese nobleman, took grand exception to Phaulkon's influence over King Narai, foreseeing a danger of the French subverting the king and the kingdom itself. He also, incidentally, wanted the throne for himself.

Constantine Phaulkon's career ended abruptly. Perhaps too conveniently, King Narai fell ill and was confined to his palace. Phra Phetraja grabbed his chance. He had the king isolated, arrested Phaulkon, and drove out the French.

King Narai died and, in a matter of days, Phra Phetraja had himself proclaimed king. He had Phaulkon beheaded, though the new king wreaked no bloody vengeance on the Greek's widow and children.

Thais regard Phra Phetraja as a hero, seeing that he saved the kingdom from Louis XIV's designs. To this day, the word *farangset* (meaning 'French') has a bad connotation to some Thais. And, unfortunately, for other whites, the *farang* part of the word has tarred all white Caucasian foreigners with the same brush. France's imperial behaviour in the nineteenth century did nothing to change Siamese opinion of what they saw as trickiness and unreliability. This was borne out by France's dismemberment of Siamese dominions when they seized Cambodia, absorbed Laos, and demanded the secession of the Lao-speaking eastern provinces of Siam, as well.

In a celebrated incident in 1893, the French attacked Siamese coastal defences at Samut Prakan and took over many Siamese posts along the Mekong River. Further, the French occupied the entire province of Chanthaburi, holding it as hostage to Siamese good behaviour and not returning it until 1907.

But let's back up a bit to two Burmese victories in the seemingly endless wars between Ayuddhaya and whoever ruled in Burma. In the 1590s, Burmese troops occupied Ayuddhaya, and a Siamese puppet king was put on the throne. The Burmese were eventually driven out by one of the princes they had taken as hostage, Naresuan (now also dubbed 'the Great'). Once again, this time in the late 1760s, the Burmese invaded in force, in a successful attempt to take Ayuddhaya.

Partly because of Ayuddhayas decadence under too-rich, too-soft kings, the Burmese succeeded in breaching the city's walls after a siege lasting nearly two years. They rushed in to sack the Siamese capital, practically dismantling it brick by brick in some places. The destruction was so great that the city never recovered its royal role and is today only a minor provincial capital among the ruins.

In those days, golden images of the Buddha, too big to hide and too heavy to move, were often coated with brick and stucco to disguise them as ordinary statues. One, said to be the largest golden Buddha image ever seen, was discovered by accident when an attempt was made to move it. The image proved far too heavy for the crane lifting it. The crane toppled over, dropping the statue. This shattered its stucco covering, revealing, after hundreds of years, its true nature. It can be seen today in Bangkok's Wat Traimitr in Chinatown (known as Yaowarat).

In the chaos of their last days, Ayuddhayans filled huge clay water jars with their domestic valuables, sealed them, and either buried them

or rolled them into the city's *khlongs* ('canals') or rivers. For nearly 200 years, amateur divers have been risking their lives to discover and salvage the jars, exposing to us the lustrous weavings, the filigree golden ornaments, and all manner of other riches of those days.

In 1970, diggers in one of the ruined Buddhist monuments uncovered a cache of golden ornaments. In this case, unlike most, these artefacts can be seen in the Ayutthaya National Museum. And the fate of other loot found by treasure seekers since then? Hidden away by finders-keepers or, unfortunately, sold on the illegal antiquities market.

The ruins of the former capital can be seen, though they are mostly brickfields and walls or towers that lean crazily. However, the palaces, offices, and the homes of ordinary people were usually built of wood or bamboo with thatched roofing, and they burned in the conflagration as the Burmese sacked and fired the city. Because the temples were often made of brick and covered with stucco, their remains stand to remind visitors of the once-greatness of the city. Ayuddhaya was, at the time, as great as Paris, and even larger than London in the days when the colonies of British North America were about to proclaim their independence.

The Burmese marched off most of the remaining Ayuddhayan population, including monks, palace musicians and dancers, official and lesser folk, each laden with some of the loot. Golden roof tiles from the temples disappeared in the march to Burma, and so did people of talent and knowledge. The blow to Siam's culture was nearly fatal. Not only did the invaders carry off items of value, but they destroyed libraries, archives, statues, and even the golden plates that had inscribed on them the names and dates of each of the Ayuddhayan kings and their reigns. With this destruction, much of Siamese history disappeared.

Even the last king disappeared. When two likely male bodies were discovered in the general ruination, both were identified as the king's. It has never been certain which of them was and which wasn't. A later king gave them each a royal cremation just to be on the safe side. Still, a rumour has always circulated that the real monarch, his identity kept secret from his Burmese captors, died of exposure and hunger on the stragglers' march to incarceration and slavery in Burma. Many Thais today still dislike the Burmese because of these wars and the destruction they caused.

One of the last generals of the Ayuddhayan forces was Phya Tak (now known as 'King Taksin the Great'). He left the doomed city when the king forbade undertaking what might have been a viable defence. He went to Chanthaburi, from that base, organized Siamese defence forces. From there he drove out the marauding Burmese, restored order, and quelled the rebellions and separatist banditry. For this he was credited

with saving the unity of the kingdom, despite having abandoned the capital city in its time of greatest need. He proclaimed himself king and established his capital in what is now Thonburi, on the west bank of the Chao Phraya facing today's Bangkok.

What happened then is not historically certain. It is a story perhaps reminiscent of that of King Richard III of England, the one Shakespeare depicted (probably erroneously) as a hunchback and plotter of the murder of his two young nephews in the Tower of London. Taksin, as we call him today, became the whipping boy and pretext for the seizure of the throne by a talented and popular military leader related to the Ayuddhayan royal house. His name was Phya Chakri, and he is the founder of the present royal dynasty and great-great-great-grandfather to the present king. He is known as King Rama I, or Phra Buddha Yodfa Chulaloke.

Chakri's supporters put it about that King Taksin had gone mad, proclaimed himself as the Buddha incarnate, and otherwise acted erratically. Chakri was 'invited' to rush back to Thonburi, where he put matters right and then acceded the throne.

In the thirty years that I have lived in Thailand, there has been a great revision of history. King Taksin has been rehabilitated and has been granted generous recognition for saving the country from the devastation and disintegration following the withdrawal of the Burmese. In the centre of a busy traffic circle in Thonburi, a great equestrian statue rears up as a monument to his good qualities as the saviour of Siam, even though he once was regarded as an unworthy usurper against the proper ruling dynasty. History has shown the dangers of keeping deposed kings about. In the end, King Taksin was disposed of by being stuffed in a velvet sack and beaten to death with a sandalwood cudgel.

From the reign of King Rama I (formerly Phya Chakri), the kings of Siam have tried to recapture the ancient culture that fell in the Burmese invasion. The capital was relocated across the Chao Phraya River to Bangkok, at that time an unimportant fishing village, but much more easily defensible from possible invaders, and given the resounding name of: Krungthepmahanakorn amornratanakosindra mahindrayudhaya mahadilokpop nopharatanarajadhaniburirom udomrajanivetmahasatharn amornphimarnavatarnsathit sakkathattiyavishnukamprasit. For sheer elegance, you will have to admit it's better than 'Village of the Wild Hog Plum,' which is what Bangkok means literally. The new and royal name has a poetic lilt to it, but is far too long to type on a business envelope.

It is preserved today in the short version, Krungthep, city of the *devas*, or angelic beings.

King Rama III, son of Rama II, tried to restore the concept of the *deva-raja*, or god-king—an Indian-Khmer idea—and kept himself from his subjects' view except in very official ceremonies. But by the time of his reign in the mid-1800s, Siam was facing problems from beyond its borders. Rifles, cannons, steam-powered warships, the electric telegraph—all of these posed threats to a country that still depended upon its elephant corps, canoes, small artillery, and magic for its defence.

This was the era when Europeans were gobbling up much of the underdeveloped world on all continents. Already, Spain and Portugal had shown the way, establishing enormous empires. France, Great Britain, and the Netherlands set up rival empires supplanting the rajas, mahârajas, nawabs, sultans, and nizams who, if they dared, fought back at their own risk.

Colonial History and the Modern Expat

As you will read many times in articles and books about this country, Thailand has never been colonized. Thais are very proud that their kingdom was never a colony of any of what we used to call the Great

Powers. Every other square foot of Southeast Asia has at one time or another been ruled by foreigners. Nor has Thailand ever been an official protectorate, a country under foreign control, but has always retained its own flag and nominal ruler.

The Thais have never experienced foreign rule directly. However, they are very much aware of its consequences, as for several hundred years they were surrounded by examples of it.

During the Second World War, the colonial overlords were defeated, and their subject colonies acquired at least nominal independence thanks to the invading Japanese. True independence took even longer, of course, as they then had to do something about the Japanese. After the war, several of the former Great Powers tried to take back their possessions, but by then the spirit of the times was against colonialism. They lost everything, except for Britain and Portugal, who held tenaciously onto Hong Kong and Macao until these colonies were returned to the awakening giant.

How Thailand managed to stay free is further discussed in this chapter. Suffice it to say that it wasn't easy, and that it has helped form the national psyche.

But before we return to the unrolling of Thai history, it would be wise to look at the modern implications of all this historical data. We need to do this since Thais react sometimes to a current event due to their own unique historical perspective—which we all do. Thais are sensitive to what they perceive as anti-Thai slights from non-Thais. That's a leftover from colonial days, when such attitudes were more common.

Colonial attitudes such as condescension toward the Thai are well  known. The white man's burden was that of civilizing the supposedly less-civilized Asians. Racism in its various forms was also implicit in the expansionism of those days.

Sometimes expats today may seem condescending or even racist. I suppose sometimes they can be. But let's rather be charitable, giving the vast majority of foreigners living here in Thailand the benefit of the doubt. What might look like racist condescension might really be something else. When expats have gripe sessions about Thais, these complaints have more to do with ignorance, fear of the unknown, or lack of awareness of language, customs, and values than they do with racism.

So it isn't just for the benefit of a better cross-cultural adjustment that we recommend acquiring as much knowledge about Thailand as possible. That's one reason we recommend learning the Thai language.

Because of their history (to which we now return after this brief digression), Thai people may sometimes still confuse lack of knowledge with racism—to the expat's detriment.

Continuing our ride through Thai history, the well-known European axiom, 'First the Cross, then the flag,' warned several Asian realms to try to ban Christian missionaries as the forerunners of treason and political invasion. The Manchus in China tried to get rid of missionaries, and put down widespread nationalistic uprisings. They ended up by losing territories (such as Hong Kong) and being forced to accept the 'Big-nosed, hairy-faced barbarians' and their opium. After the Boxer Rebellion in China, the ancient dynasty fell. In 1911, a republic, this time Chinese, was proclaimed.

Change was everywhere, and almost none of it was advantageous to Asians anywhere. As King Rama IV of Siam put it to Christian missionaries: "Bring us your education and your hospitals, but keep your superstitions to yourself. We have our own."

The missionaries came to Siam and established hospitals, orphanages, and schools that still operate today. They were also responsible for the first Thai-language printing press and typewriter, from which they cut two letters out of the Thai alphabet to accommodate the rest to the keys available. The combined European and American influence also resulted in changes of dress, food, customs, and architecture.

As happened elsewhere in Asia, laws were even forced on Siam. At that time, the country had no formal codified law. Almost all of it was built on the royal will expressed in edicts, or on remembered local practices and customs, like the common law of England. The Europeans found it difficult to deal with this situation and demanded for their subjects the right of extraterritoriality in Siam, meaning that a foreigner could not be tried in a Siamese court but only in a consular court of his own nationality and under his nation's laws. Thus, British subjects, in whatever clash they'd had with each other or with the Siamese, would only be heard in a British consular court, French citizens in a French consular court, and so on.

In time, the US and almost all European powers involved in Siam enjoyed this right. In effect, they were not subject to Siamese law at all. Where this was very wrong, in the Siamese government's view, was that the British claimed that not only were all their subjects covered by this right, but even their colonials—so that Indians, Malays, Burmese, and Hong Kong Chinese could be prosecuted in Siam only by the British consul. The French, too, claimed that all Vietnamese, Cambodians, Laotians, and Pondichéry Indians were to be protected as French. This so compromised Siam's sovereignty that about the only people who were subject to its courts and laws were the Siamese and various other (generally Asian) citizens—and then only if they were not in dispute with any person, institution, or company that was protected by the extraterritoriality agreements. China and Japan, too, were forced to accept this concept, which they regarded as humiliating and harmful to their own national interests.

Because of this, many Thais objected to their country siding with the colonial oppressors (Great Britain and France) in the First World War. Those with wider experience of the world accepted King Rama VI's argument that, as an ally of the Allies, Siam would be counted among the victors and enjoy recognition as an independent nation at the considerations that ended with the Treaty of Versailles in 1919. This proved to be the case. The United States was the first developed Western country to give up extraterritoriality in Siam, which they did in the 1920s. Since this was after the First World War, in which Siam had participated by sending a flying corps and labour gangs to France, perhaps it was a reward for being on the winning side.

By siding with the Allies and becoming one of them, Siam could now legally take over properties and ships of the Central Powers, now enemy aliens—Germany, Austria-Hungary, Bulgaria, and the Ottoman Empire—and end whatever capitulations Siam may have had to grant to those countries.

From the second half of the nineteenth century, Siam was under pressure on almost all fronts. Sir John Bowring's treaty of 1855 forced the kingdom to open its markets to free trade, which gave British merchants free access to Siamese markets, thus ending the exclusive royal monopoly on foreign trade. Britain was the first to force this concession. Then other countries accorded treaty status got the same rights. Rather than garner high profit on this trade, the agreements limited the Siamese to the imposition of a duty on all imported goods of not more than three percent.

The effect was to revolutionize tax collection in Siam and to set the stage for many more modernizations to come—in the reigns of King Rama IV (1854-1868) and his son Rama V (1868-1910), respectively called Mongkut and Chulalongkorn by the foreigners. (These are the king and young crown prince of *The King and I*.)

Looking back at subsequent developments, it is hard to believe that the Thais were so forward-looking that one of the products they wanted to reserve all trading in was rice. A very few decades later, rice and teak exports were financing most Siamese trade. It was the most important source of wealth until tourism overtook it in money value only in recent years.

The governments of these two kings had to virtually reinvent the administrative structure of the kingdom, set up military and police hierarchies in their modern form, and abolish those practices—like slavery—that threatened to provoke foreign interference in domestic affairs. At the same time, European powers were nibbling off chunks of the kingdom to add to their neighbouring colonial possessions. Siam employed an old and effective survival policy, 'bend like the bamboo in the storm,' and so managed to give up a little in order to not get swallowed whole.

Part of avoiding unwanted colonial occupation was using the rivalry between Great Britain and France, which had been going on for more than a century around the world. France and Great Britain, to avoid damaging clashes between themselves, made an agreement to leave at least a nominally independent slice of Siam along the Chao Phraya river valley.

The last land grabs were those of 1904 and 1907 by France, and 1910 by Britain. It was those areas, as well as one in the northeast of Burma, that were subject to Siamese claims in the Second World War, and led to the change of the kingdom's name from Siam to Thailand.

By the time of the death of the much-loved King Chulalongkorn (Rama V) in 1910, the kingdom's borders were fairly clearly defined, much as they are today, and many other matters could be attended to. These included the laying of railway lines, stringing telegraph and telephone wires, and the establishment of the electric tramways in Bangkok, which were the first in Asia. Opium consumption was forbidden, and the police force was ordered to wear shoes. This sort of reform led to what many regarded as excessive changes, particularly after the 'revolution' of 1932.

During the reigns of King Rama VI, called Vajiravudh and Mongkut Klao (1910-1925) and his brother, Rama VII, Prajadhipok or Pok Klao (1925-1935), a flood of changes began to erode traditional Thai ways. Some of these were: the adoption of surnames (before this, no Thai had a last name); older Siamese styles replaced by Western dress; required use of spoons and forks at the table instead of fingers; sitting on chairs rather than on floors or mats; the popular advent of cinema and radio; initiating and standardizing education in schools for all children of both sexes; displacing traditional herbal medicines and their practitioners with Western-style doctors and hospitals; the building of motorable streets and roads, which led to cars increasing in number; the introduction of marriage and criminal codes based on Western models; revising the Thai alphabet and dropping some redundant letters; sending youths overseas for education; revising and enlarging government bureaucracy; the establishment of an academy for training staff for government service (this eventually became Chulalongkorn University); and extending postal and telegraph services into more outlying areas.

In the late 1920s this reformism spread even further and led to the 'revolution' of June 24th, 1932. Its unexpected result was the ending of centuries of absolute monarchy.

Ancient Siam Disappears, Thailand Is Born

In 1932 a group of Siamese who had studied in France and Great Britain resented what they considered to be the overweening rule of the king and his family (in particular his ultra-conservative elder uncles). Pridi Banomyong (or Phanomyong) was a young lawyer with the royal title of Luang Pradit Manudham. He studied in France, where he ran around with other Siamese who were also disenchanted with the king's absolute power.

Pridi took up with several others, including a military man by the name of Plaek Phibunsongkhram. Their 'revolution' presented the king (Prajadhipok, Rama VII) with a draft of a new constitution and a threat that if he did not acquiesce, the monarchy might be abolished.

King Rama VII, who was at Hua Hin, south of Bangkok on the Gulf of Siam, studied his options. He might try to fight the upstarts, thus plunging the kingdom into a bloody conflict with an unknowable outcome. Or he could accept the challenge of introducing democracy under his own guidance. This latter option was more appealing, mostly because he had been

19

planning to do so anyway. He chose to give in to the demands pressed upon him, including the proclamation of a constitution—Siam's first.

Things did not work out well. In 1934 the king left Siam for eye treatment abroad and eventually abdicated while in England. This left Pridi and Plaek to face it off. Pridi was accused of leftist leanings, particularly in his economic reform plans; Plaek was a military nationalist who had a very different agenda.

King Rama VII was the last of the absolute monarchs and would have been the first of the constitutional kings, had he not been virtually forced to leave Siam and then to abdicate. His uncles opposed his granting a democratic constitution. They opposed the constitution even though it remained royalist in character, with the king retaining major power. The royal uncles' intransigence is what prevented a compromise between the king and the rebellious groups and forced him to leave the country.

King Rama VII had no direct heirs, so it was to the great happiness of the plotters and rebels that the throne then fell to his young nephew, Ananda Mahidol, a grandson of King Rama V. This young man became King Rama VIII and acceded the throne while still a teenager at school in Switzerland. Siam, or Thailand as it was known from 1939-1945, then endured a minority rule under a regency in a confused time of shifts and struggles made worse by the worldwide economic depression and then the Second World War.

The boy king 'reigned' from halfway around the world, while Pridi was made regent. Plaek, who was prime minister, allied Thailand with the Axis Powers (Germany, Italy, Hungary, Romania, and Japan) and declared war, first on France (the Indochina War of short duration that ended with Japan's arbitration) and later, on Great Britain and the United States.

The government declared war on the US, but the Thai ambassador in Washington deliberately failed to deliver the declaration, a typically Thai way of negotiating troubled waters by 'doing' and 'not doing' at the same time. Thus, after the war, the US did not regard Thailand as an enemy power, although Great Britain did.

When military affairs started to go badly for Japan, the new prime minister quietly arrested Plaek, the former pro-Japanese prime minister, and withdrew from the alliance. Meanwhile, there had been an active Free Thai movement that consisted of guerrilla fighters and spies organized and paid for by the Allies. (Pridi, code-named 'Ruth,' ran the Thai end of the Free Thai from the regent's office right under the noses of the Japanese.) The Free Thai became more visible as the Axis fell into increasing disfavour. Changing its name back to Siam and being willing to return territories occupied as 'Thailand,' Siam yet again successfully employed its ancient policy of bending with the wind, like a bamboo in a tempest. As the US had not reciprocated Thailand's declaration of war, the kingdom was able to avoid some of the post-war tangle it had with Great Britain, which considered it a defeated enemy.

After the war, King Rama VIII paid only one brief visit to Siam, where he was enthusiastically received by the populace. As he had not yet finished his studies, it was necessary for him to return to Switzerland. Preparations were being made for his departure for Europe with his mother and younger brother when he was found dead of a gunshot wound in the palace, under circumstances that have never been fully explained.

When the young King Ananda was found dead, Plaek blamed Pridi. Pridi and one of his principal followers had to flee—with American and British collaboration.

Despite a movement to bring Pridi home, he died overseas. His family, however, lives in Bangkok quite unmolested, as does that of the aide to Pridi, who fled to live in Macao. Plaek resumed power until a botched attempt at twisting an election led to his flight to Japan, from where he never returned.

In 1946, King Rama VIII was succeeded by his younger brother, Bhumiphol Adulyadej, the present king (Rama IX).

It might be well to explain to expats that, although these events occurred over fifty years ago, it is considered extremely inappropriate for *farang* to speculate about the death of King Rama VIII. It is not even written about or referred to by Thais. One might add that the musical film, *The King and I*, starring Yul Brynner, was banned in Thailand because of its simplistic and impolite depiction of the much-respected Rama IV, King Mongkut, and the royal family. The 1946 film, *Anna and the King of Siam*, with Rex Harrison as the king, was not officially banned, but it was not shown in the cinemas of Thailand.

After the Second World War, change continued on all fronts. Remember that for 100 years, Thais had been under pressure to alter one thing or another in their culture and ways. During his long reign (1868-1910), as King Rama V made treaties to fend off European rapacity, he instituted reforms. European-style uniforms for the military and police made an appearance, and women were commanded to wear blouses instead of scarves or sarong-like tops they had worn before. The traditional lower garment was retained. This is the *chongkraben*, a long piece of cloth gathered to the front, with the extra cloth rolled, and then drawn between the legs and tucked up the back.

During King Rama VI's reign, reforms gathered speed. A royal pages' school was opened to train candidates for the government bureaucracy, and many Thais were sent off to Europe to study subjects thought useful for the development of the kingdom. One prince sailed off to study the British military; another to Germany to study naval affairs; one to Russia to live at the Tsar's court, and so on.

Prince Mahidol, the future father of kings Rama VIII and IX, went to study medicine and returned as a well-trained doctor. While overseas, he met his future wife, a commoner. She became, from the 1920s on, one of the most revered and loved people in the Chakri dynasty. She was the Princess Mother, whose death in 1995 caused nationwide grief.

The king had to develop a loyal bureaucratic class to help him with his planned reforms. King Rama V not only sent his sons off to become familiar with modern ideas, he also invited foreign experts to help build his army, his navy, and a railway system to meet the economic and military needs of the realm. British, German, Belgian, and Danish firms were prominent in the railways, the electric tramway, and in various other infrastructural improvements. Because there were few Siamese trained for management jobs, foreigners often found themselves running sections of the government. This situation led to some resentment, as it had in the seventeenth century with the Greek, Constantine Phaulkon, although this time no one ended up beheaded.

A good example of the management roles filled by foreigners was Francis B. Sayre, the son-in-law of US president Woodrow Wilson, who aided the Siamese foreign affairs ministry in getting rid of the extra-territoriality agreements that had proved so vexing to the government officers. Another example was a Dutchman, J. Homan van der Heide, who helped plan a massive and imaginative hydraulic system, involving rivers and *khlongs*, to assure year-round water sufficiency for agriculture and internal navigation. The British, in control of the kingdom's finances, unfortunately managed to derail that ambitious plan. It threatened interests of their own, and so Thailand is still to this day trying to solve its water problems upcountry.

The French helped by setting up and teaching classes in international political relations, and even convinced the Siamese to agree to let French be the language of instruction!

But probably the most important reform of King Rama V's reign was the abolition of slavery, without the civil strife that occurred in the US. This programme succeeded without a shot being fired, as Thais are proud to point out. To tell the truth, without detracting from King Rama V's magnificently successful and peaceful reform, the institution of slavery was not all that important to the economy of the kingdom. From the earliest moments of his reign, in 1868, the king decreed that no children were to be born into slavery ever again. A traditional source of slaves had been debtors, who often sold themselves or other family members to clear their debts. The king abolished that, as well. Additionally, Siam fought no foreign wars during this period, so no prisoners of war were forced into servitude, as had been the traditional practice throughout the region.

By the time of total abolition in 1905, only aged family retainers remained in servitude, and the abolition made little difference to their well-being. It impressed the foreigners, though, who might otherwise have believed they should step in to rectify this ancient and no-longer-acceptable practice.

The fear of the various expanding colonial powers forced many countries to make reforms deemed necessary by those very colony-seeking nations. There was a threat that if the 'lesser countries' failed to carry out the reforms, the colonialists would step in and do it themselves—with unnamed, but imaginable results. Whereas it had at one time been 'First the Cross, then the flag,' it became, in the time of most-active colony seeking, 'First trade and then control.' Siam was very fortunate in avoiding the most obvious forms of colonization.

'Free trade!' was the clarion call of capitalist Great Britain and, to a lesser extent, of the other European states involved in the region. The US was also afraid of being left out.

Cultural influences are today pressing on the Thais. The movies and television programming have had a tremendous effect on dress, music, dance, and youthful fashions and behaviour. Hardly any aspect of Thai life has escaped these changes: cheeseburgers, pizzas, cakes, and pastries are washed down with milk, fizzy drinks, and new alcoholic beverages. Cigarettes have all but replaced the chewing of *maak*, the concoction of betel leaves, areca nuts, lime paste, and other goodies that leave blood-like stains wherever spat. As the Europeans gave up bustles and hoop skirts for ever more modern clothing, so the Thais rushed to change the *chongkraben* and *pha sin* (a long formal skirt) to mini-skirts; flowers in the hair to hats—by government command. The Thai woman's foot went from bare, or sandal-like slip-your-toes-in flip-flops, to high-heels and wedgies. Cars replaced motorbikes, which had replaced bicycles, which in turn had replaced buffalo carts, rickshaws, and elephants. These changes took place all over Siam, and continue in modern Thailand to this day.

Even intimate matters have been exposed and changed. Once poly-gynous, today Thai men may register their marriages at a rate of only 'one per province.' As Thailand has 76 provinces, they are not too limited. But a modern threat hangs over polygyny—that of installing a central computer-based registry for citizen ID cards that will show in the code exactly how many wives a man has at the time he proposes to take a new one. This will not end multiple marriages, of course, but may slow down the defrauding of women by much-married males.

During the period before the Second World War, and again four years later, the name of the kingdom was changed from Siam to Thailand, to the distress of much of today's tourist industry that finds the first moniker more romantic and appealing. Actually, Thailand is much closer to what the Thais, in their own language, call themselves: *muang Thai*, *khon Thai* or 'Thai-land' and 'Thai people.' King Rama VI ordered the nation's flag changed from the old white-elephant-on-a-scarlet-field to today's familiar red, white, and blue stripes. It is said the king disliked having an animal on the flag because "no civilized country" had such a standard.

There is an anecdote to the effect that when Sir John Bowring com-posed his famous treaty of 1855 to force the kingdom to open to British commerce, he reasonably enquired into the name of the signatory country with which he was negotiating. No Thai could enlighten him. While Sir John could call his country, a realm under Queen Victoria, the United Kingdom of Great Britain and Ireland (as it was then), the Thais had no simple equivalent. There were two Thai kings simultaneously, something that confused foreigners no end, and a suggestion to use the name of the era, Ratanakosin, failed to clear things up. Finally, Sir John, in a fit of red-faced pique (it was hot on his quarterdeck, perhaps), turned to his Malay interpreter and demanded the name of this country. "Sayam," the interpreter said. Sir John re-spelled it as 'Siam,' had it entered in the treaty, and the Siamese politely accepted it as the English name of their country. So Siam it remained until changed for the last time in 1949 to Thailand. It is possible of course that you may hear of, or read, other explanations for the name of Siam, but Sir John's is good enough for me.

Dictatorship and War

During the dictatorship of Field Marshal Plaek Phibunsongkhram, between the late 1930s and the end of the Second World War, when he was denounced as a war criminal, and then during his return to power in the mid-1940s until the end of his era in 1959, even the alphabet was reformed somewhat.

Among the many modernizations Plaek insisted upon were that women wear hats and let down their *chongkraben* into skirts; that men wear Western-styled suits and ties (in total disregard of the climate); and that everyone stop chewing *maak*.

At one time, Siamese women cut their hair flat-top style; later it had to be permed and frizzy; and even later, severely bobbed. Men let theirs grow until there was opposition to hippy styles and the government strongly suggested shorter hair.

The period of the Second World War is the setting for the famous movie, *The Bridge on the River Kwai* (as the French author of the original book spelled the name of the river). This horrifying account of the construction through the jungle of a railway to allow the Imperial Japanese Army to ship men and supplies from Siam into Burma seems, over the years, to lose no interest for readers of the book or viewers of the film. It has been more than fifty years since the end of the Pacific War, yet people still come to see the bridge and what's left of the Death Railway. They don't appear to care much that the bridge they see is a post-war replacement for the original that was bombed by the Allies (and not blown up, as in the movie).

Every year in late November and early December there is a ten-day-long fair at the bridge, with an impressive nightly *son et lumière* performance on the construction and destruction of the span.

The war's end found Thailand facing a number of bruising problems, including British demands for reparations. With the arrest of pro-Axis Field Marshal Plaek, the Thais could once again work two ends against the middle. They disowned the declaration of war against the US (which

had not accepted it as the "will of the Thai people" anyway) and thus received American support against British demands. That the exiled field marshal could later come back to power for a few more years only proves the fluid nature of Thai politics.

After the war, Thailand faced an insurgency said by the government to be communist-inspired or at least financially supported. Others claimed that the rebels were anti-military-dictatorship rather than particularly pro-communist. The suppression of this movement, whichever it really was, permitted the right-wing regimes of posturing military officers to screw down their rule on the Thais. Generals took turns acting as prime minister, with the odd, short-lived civilian government permitted every once in a while.

In 1950, Thailand was urged by the US to join the United Nations' forces in the Korean War. Although almost no one remembers it, Thailand was the third-heaviest contributor of troops to that war. The Thai government responded to the challenge of keeping the communist menace at a distance, much as the Americans were doing. Today, after subsequent wars in Southeast Asia, with the fall of Vietnam, Laos, and Cambodia to the communists in 1975, this policy looks less naïve than many Thai critics thought it at the time.

Because I had already studied Thai and Chinese during my university years at Berkeley and had already been to Asia, when my turn for military service came up, I was sent to Tokyo as a psychological warfare specialist. With this luminous title emblazoned on my uniform, I was assigned to take care of the Southeast Asian countries in the psy-war unit. My daily work consisted of reading newspapers to seek out items that might show these countries' interest in and support of the American-led United Nations efforts in Korea.

While this is not meant to be a war story of my own, it is pertinent. I had teeth problems. An infection set into the roots of one tooth and then spread to the next. The medics finally determined to hospitalize me to prevent further damage. The hospital was set up for injuries to soldiers' skulls and other terrible facial damage, amongst which my case seemed a bit lacking in urgency. Lying in bed, I had nothing better to do than read and notice my fellow ward mates. One day, the patient nearest to me lay back on his stacked pillows, singing away and looking at a large-page photo magazine. I glanced at it and then sat up so abruptly that my own pillows and books tumbled from my bed to the floor. The magazine was in Thai! I worked out that it dealt with the young king and his new bride. There was a full-page picture of the royal couple being received by a deliriously happy public. In my concentration, I didn't notice that the soldier, an Asian, had stopped singing and had signalled his Asian companion in the next bed to come over. The two of them then stared at me over the top edge of the magazine page.

I was anything but fluent in speaking the language. However, I had retained enough from classroom days to carry on very basic communications. Our conversation interested the rest of our ward mates, who later interrogated me about the two Asians. "Who are they? Whose army are they in? Why are they in here with us?

They were Thai sailors, in the hospital for wounds suffered aboard their ship. There were many Thai soldiers there, too, suffering from frostbite.

Now that I have lived in Thailand for more than thirty years, I am sorry that long ago I lost the picture and address of Sergeant Yod from Phetburi or Rajburi. Yod was, except for the two sailors in my hospital ward, the first Thai I had ever met.

Yod was a likeable man. We spent many hours together in his ward, chatting about our different worlds, lives, hopes, and fears. Sitting around, sopping up our conversations, were the other Thais, every one suffering the ugly process of losing fingers, ears, noses, lips, cheeks, and toes to the gangrene that can follow frostbite. (Until sent to Korea, these young men from the provinces of Central Siam had never seen ice outside of a refrigerator or lying about in a saw-dusted block, ready to be crushed for drinks.)

It wasn't long until I came to love those men, cheerful even under these awful circumstances. Yod convinced me that while he could never save enough money to visit me in California, I might some day find my way to Thailand. My interest in these people led the Thai Embassy nurse to mention me to their air attaché, who one day came to the hospital to invite me to fly to Thailand on one of the courier flights.

How I wish I had taken the Royal Thai Air Force up on that invitation. The year was 1952—the great changes that would alter the face of Bangkok were just starting. But unfortunately, I hadn't saved enough of my meagre soldier's pay to afford the trip, even with the generous offer of free transportation. When the Korean action ended for me, I didn't go to Thailand. I didn't seek out Yod. It took me a dozen more years to make it to Thailand. Since then, aside from little holiday trips, here I have stayed—attracted by three of the qualities this land affords: the climate, the food, and the people.

After the Second World War, Thailand faced even more changes. For one thing, it became better known internationally. One of the early leaders of the new United Nations was a Thai prince, Wan Waithayakorn. As foreign minister, Prince Wan Waithayakorn was instrumental in getting the country into the United Nations right from its beginning. Later, when the UN was still quite new, he was president of the General Assembly. He was in the news quite often during that period.

With more frequent airline services, tourism caught on and foreigners, a few thousands at first, then millions, began to arrive. Japanese investment helped the economy turn from agriculture to industry, gradually shifting the source of wealth from rice to more diversified national products such as teak, rosewood, tapioca, maize, gemstones, and such. The war in Vietnam also played a role in bringing on a boom in the Thai economy.

Yet the Thai government remained conservative and repressive in its bureaucratic dead weight. This went on for years until students rose up in 1973 and overthrew the 'Three Tyrants': Thanom Kittikachorn and his son Narong, and Praphas Charusathien, who had for years refused to grant a constitution. Even the king's mediation could not forestall a police attack on the protestors that killed hundreds. Residents of Bangkok at that time can still remember the picture of one dead student being carried away by her friends. The flag they had wrapped around her was soaked a brilliant red. But the government of what an expat journalist termed "The Father, Son, and Wholly Gross" was overturned.

All through the Vietnam War, American military personnel were routinely assigned short holidays to Bangkok—five days of R & R, at the end of which they'd be flown back to the carnage. Many Thai businesses thrived because of that war, among them bars and houses of prostitution.

A new term entered the Thai vocabulary: *mia chao*, the 'hired wife'—a Thai woman enjoying a long-term business arrangement with a foreigner in what someone described as "stretched-out prostitution."

At the time, most Thais supported the official American position that the fighting was to prevent the 'domino theory' from coming true. This concept held that the communists would eventually take over the governments of Vietnam, Laos, Cambodia, and then possibly attempt to 'liberate' Thailand and Burma, as well.

If the Americans' goal in the war was to keep South Vietnam free of the communists, they failed. The American military's withdrawal left South Vietnam to its fate. This fact shook many Thais' faith in Americans, which was rattled further when the Americans reacted belligerently to an incident involving the *Mayaguez*, a freighter that had been forced into a Cambodian port. As the Americans saw it, it had been hijacked by the Khmers, and they were prepared to use force to free it. This came close to involving the Thais—as allies of the Americans and owners of the base the Americans used in their military action—in a possible shooting match with Cambodia.

A new government under Mom Rajavong Kukrit Pramoj told the American military to go home. They did, and it has always embarrassed me that the only Thais who were vocal in their opposition to the American withdrawal seemed to me to be *samlor* drivers and prostitutes.

When the Cold War ended with the collapse of the Soviet Union, and with the waves of liberalization that periodically temper the Chinese communists, Thais felt safe to follow their own interests, paying less attention to the desires and policies of the former Great Powers. Extraterritoriality was already a thing of the near-forgotten past; no longer did Thais kowtow to self-important Westerners or East Asians. They seemed more aware of their own problems, such as the decay of the environment, the negative effects of mass tourism, and the realization of their own goals in the region and on the world stage.

ASEAN, the Association of Southeast Asian Nations (originally Thailand, Malaysia, Singapore, Indonesia, and the Philippines, then later joined by Brunei, Vietnam, Cambodia, Laos, and Burma), was but one example of the new Thai policy of co-operation with countries of this region. Thai democracy appears more firmly established, although it is still fragile and never totally free of the shadow of military adventurism and coup making that has characterized much of its recent past.

It is interesting that in Thai, 'democracy' means *a limitation of the powers of an absolute monarch*. This was what was achieved in 1932. When the military government was overthrown in 1973 after that explosion of violence, peace was restored, and much of the credit was given to the king. At that time, despite (or because of) the lack of a constitution, His Majesty commanded that a 2,347-member consultative assembly be called, and set up an appointed interim government until a new constitution could be prepared. Few Thais criticized this exercise of extra constitutional royal power. In fact, most of them approved of the king's involvement. They felt fortunate that Thailand had a reigning monarch who was unafraid to exercise unwritten royal prerogatives to preserve peace in the kingdom.

In 1976, when military dictatorship again was imposed, it was after a suppression of student demonstrations even bloodier than that in 1973. It involved right-wing mobs, in addition to police and soldiers, who clubbed to death students (protesters and non-protesters alike) who were taking refuge in Thammasat University.

In 1991, the most recent military coup took place, and the elected civilian government was overthrown by the military because of "massive corruption." This led to another bloody confrontation in 1992 at the Democracy Monument. Again, hundreds if not thousands of Thais were killed and wounded, although this time some elements of the military refused to participate in the suppression. The army backed down, however, and some generals were retired from positions of influence. Elections were held and a new civilian government came about, lasting until early 1995, when its prime minister dissolved parliament and ordered new elections.

The king's intervention to end the confrontation of 1992 was highly publicized. His Majesty commanded the leaders of the two major factions to attend upon him, and on worldwide television the dissident political leader and the army supreme commander (and would-be prime minister) were seen crawling on their knees and elbows before the Thai king. It was an exhilarating moment for Thais and a puzzling one for many foreign viewers that, in this age of republics and dictatorships, a constitutional monarch could command such voluntary respect and obedience from his subjects.

A final word: I have mentioned the three factors that have kept me in Thailand: the climate, the food (to my mind, the most delicious cuisine on earth), and the people. However, every December I complain about our fierce winters, when I have to pull socks on my normally bare feet at home, and wish the sarongs I ordinarily now wear were made of wool. As for the Thai people I have come to know and love, I pray I may be permitted to live among them until I die.

So much for the personal notice. I mention all this to help offset, at least in part, what might seem like negatives in some aspects of living here in Thailand. I also mention my own history because it's quite possible that you will find Thailand and Thai people equally appealing for yourself!

Politics aside and uneven economic development overlooked for the moment, the Thai people as a whole still smile; are hospitable, helpful, and generous; and find fun in whatever they do. Thailand is a country with a colourful history, an interesting present, and perhaps a splendid future.

Who Steers the Ship of State?
Government, Monarchy,
and Bureaucracy

Understanding the Thai Government

From ancient times, Siam was an absolute monarchy, which is to say that it was ruled by kings whose will was law. This system ended with the 'revolution' of 1932, and the constitution that followed resulted in the creation of a constitutional monarchy.

'Constitution' here refers to the body of law that describes the organization of the state and the king, the prime minister and his cabinet, a parliament—consisting in Thailand of an upper and a lower house with their respective duties and powers set out—and the rights and duties of citizens. Under the 1932 constitution, the king became the head of state, as distinct from the head of government, the prime minister.

It wasn't easy to work out all the arrangements and balance the various entities—executive, legislative, judiciary, and the military—and Thailand has since had some difficulty in arriving at a workable balance among all these various elements. The shift from being an agricultural state to an industrializing country has also caused many imbalances among social groups.

An intense struggle between reformers and conservatives has at times been complicated by the efforts of some individuals simply to grab power for themselves. Between 1932 and 1995 Thailand had 14 constitutions and 21 prime ministers, under three kings. In the political instability that marks Thailand's recent history, a pattern of periodic coups emerges.

The King

To this day, the king is sacred and inviolable in his person and rank, but his role in politics is constitutionally limited. Rather like Queen Elizabeth II of the United Kingdom, the king may be consulted, may advise, and may warn the government. In both countries, the monarch signs bills passed by parliament that then become law, but it is a duty

of the prime minister to countersign these documents to make them valid.

The king must be a Buddhist as well as a supporter of all religions, holding tradition as his strong point. There is a special language employed to or of him called *rajasap*. It is based on Sanskrit and Khmer, and Thai children study some of it in school.

The king is advised on his duties by a privy council of men he deems worthy of this trust. These men represent a wide range of experience and are not limited to politicians.

In international affairs the king represents the country, receiving and dispatching ambassadors, as well as receiving and sending official state visitors. He also signs the appointments of senators and commissioned officers of the army, navy, air force, and police. A peculiarly personal duty of the king has been to award degrees to university and academy graduates. As this job has become more time consuming, it has been shared out among other members of the royal family.

The king has many ceremonial functions. You will see this as you read the newspapers or watch the evening television news. The present king and queen have interested themselves in many projects among the populace, and are often seen presiding over or participating in these affairs.

The royal succession today passes from father to child, but in the past a royal council would choose the successor to the throne from among the eligible Chakri princes. The palace law now also permits succession by females. Since King Chulalongkorn's reign, the succession must be determined by the rules of primogeniture (order of birth). In the past century or so, the succession has followed this sequence:

Rama IV (1851–1868), also known to Thais as Phra Chom Klao and to foreigners as Mongkut, his princely name. He was succeeded by his son. It was this king who determined to re-name his dynastic ancestors as 'Rama' for the convenience of foreigners. This practice continues.

Rama V (1868–1910), also known to Thais as Phra Chula Chom Klao and to foreigners as Chulalongkorn. He was succeeded by his son.

Rama VI (1910–1925), also known to Thais as Phra Mongkut Klao and to foreigners as Vajiravudh, his name as a prince. As a princess was his only offspring, he was succeeded by his younger brother.

Rama VII (1925–1934 when he abdicated). He died in 1941 in England. He is known as Phra Pok Klao, and his princely name was Prajadhipok. As he had no heirs, he was succeeded by a nephew.

Rama VIII (1934–1946), also known by his name Ananda Mahidol. He was found shot to death in his palace bedroom and was succeeded by his younger brother. His death and the etiquette surrounding discussion of it are explored in the first chapter.

Rama IX (1946-present) is also known by his personal name, Bhumiphol Adulyadej. There are several ways to Romanize his name depending upon which system is used. His queen is named Sirikit. Their four children (now all adults) are their royal highnesses Princess Ubonratana, Crown Prince Vajiralongkorn, Princess Maha Chakri Sirindhorn, and Princess Chulabhornvalailaksana.

The Prime Minister

The prime ministers of Thailand since the 1932 coup that constitutionalized the government have either been elected or appointed with the consent of parliament. On occasion, they have simply presented themselves. Most have been from the army, depending upon the political situation at the time.

Except for those who present themselves for appointment as a result of a coup, prime ministers have arisen from parliament, where they are usually the head of the largest political party, the one with the most elected seats. Or they may be accepted by enough members of the parliament to lead a coalition of parties that will represent a majority of members of parliament. This has been the case most recently.

Several experiments have been carried out to set up a single-chamber parliament, an all-elected assembly, a partly-appointed, partly-elected house, or a two-house parliament (as at present) with the lower house elected and with appointed senators in the upper house. Voting age for Thais is 18 years. The generally malleable quality of Thai social and political elements reflect the continual struggles of various groups to keep or win political representation and power.

Under the prime minister is the cabinet, representing the various parties in parliament. Some are outsiders, unelected to parliament but appointed to their posts. The cabinet (of not more than 49 members) meets periodically to study proposed law and proclamations, endorsing them or not. The cabinet consists of ministers in various fields, deputy ministers, and ministers of the Prime Minister's Office. The ministries are entrusted with certain facets, such as Interior (concerning local government, census, police, censorship, citizenship, immigration, and the like), Agriculture and Co-operatives, Commerce, Trade, Public Health, Foreign Affairs, Labour, Finance, Communications and Transportation, Justice, and Education and Religious Affairs. The exact number of ministries varies as old ones are dissolved and new ones established. There are new ministries for Tourism and Sports, Social Development and Human Security, National Resources and Environment, and Information and Communications Technology, for example.

The prime minister has the right to dismiss the cabinet in part or in whole and to dissolve the parliament, thus calling for new national elections within ninety days. These are usually marred by corruption, vote-buying, occasional assassinations, and general political uproar. The Thai electorate supported 44 political parties at one time, several of them representing the interests of individual powerful politicians. The parties often dissolve themselves or merge with another and re-appear under new names. This fluidity also contributes to the malleability of Thai politics.

'Democracy' is a battered word in Thailand, despite its original meaning of a limitation of the absolute power of kings. It has not been easy for the kingdom to develop a settled arrangement that everyone will be happy to accept, as democracy is a term that probably will never be defined here exactly as it is in Western societies.

A word about the role of the Thai military in politics is in order. The army (and the air force to a greater degree, with the navy to a lesser degree) is more independent than is usual in most Western countries, and rarely has been amenable to being subject to civilian governments. It often appears to have its own agenda, made stronger in times when civilian institutions are weakest.

The Royal Thai Police is a paramilitary organization, also with its own separate agenda and power base, though technically it is under the Interior Ministry. The police have at times exercised considerable political weight and, at one point, a police general demanded the rank of field marshal. His ambition was rejected, and he died in exile in Japan, the traditional happy hunting ground for exiled politicos from Thailand.

General Organization

Unlike the United States, which uses a federal system, Thailand is a unitary state divided (from larger units to small) into *changwat* ('provinces'), *amphur* ('districts'), *tambon* ('sub-districts', also spelled *tambol*) and *muu baan* ('village clusters'). There may be other divisions for special purposes, such as *sukhaphiban* ('sanitary districts'). As towns grow into cities, the smaller districts are merged and may bear the names of traditional features such as canals (*khlong*), bridges (*saphan*), palaces (*wang*), temples (*wat*) forts (*pom*), markets (*talaat*), and docks and piers (*tha, tha ruea*). The names will persist to give hints of a colourful past.

Government Services

The Thai government operates many social services. These include the post office, telegraph and telephone, and certain telecommunications systems. It also includes prisons, some hospitals, and most primary schools. Some industries were originally started by the government because of a general lack of capital (or interest) amongst the public. The railways, some of the bus systems, a shipping company, and some truck services are all examples of Thai government organizations or state-owned enterprises. These either directly use civil servants or sub-contract through various corporations promoted and constructed by the government. They are then sometimes spun off into quasi-independent enterprises.

There are government banks and finance companies, electricity producers, water boards, museums, and golf courses. A few temples serve government activities in such ways as providing funerals for public figures. The government, rather than the private sector, has built the basic infrastructure of the kingdom.

The national parks and forests, irrigation works, and even a few hotels belong directly to the government. This is also true of airports, seaports, and the services they require. In recent years, there has been a tendency toward disinvolvement on the part of the government through privatization. Prior to the financial crisis that hit in mid-1997, the private sector was booming with a rate of growth that most Western countries envy, and local investors were happy to take over some government enterprises. After a period of adjustment, the economy has started recovering with new zeal.

While there are many NGOs in Thailand, several social organizations were started by the government and then left to sink or float on their own. While governments are often criticized for their handling of these affairs, it is probably true that, at the time, there was need for government financing for the organization to be set up.

Nowadays, with great development in capital markets, banks, insurance companies, and industries, the government is not the leader in new

projects that it used to be. In other words, where the government alone once gathered the fuel and set the fire, others now have to tend the flames and boil the rice.

Government Paperwork

Every Thai from age 15 up to seventy must have a *bat prachachon*, (citizen's 'identity card') which, by law, he or she must always carry. This card acts as legal identification and, now that it has been computerized, shows marital status and other personal details.

This ID card is based on the *thabian baan* ('household registration'), which is kept in the district office of each person's birthplace, though copies may be kept for various purposes: enrolling in school, voting, requesting a visa or passport, opening a bank account, obtaining a driver's licence, and 101 other things for which a person may need ID. At present, the household registration is computerized and online nationwide. A Thai who loses an ID card does not have to report it to the police (although they can if they wish), but can report directly to their district office. Upcountry Thais who work in Bangkok can apply for a new ID card in the capital without the need to travel back home.

The household registration sheet is an ongoing census. When a Thai is born, his or her name is entered on this sheet; when he or she moves away, he or she must withdraw the particulars from one sheet and enter it on the registration for the new address. When a person changes status from civilian to military, or vice-versa, or from monk to layman, this information is entered on the registration sheet. The same happens with marital and divorce details. The document also shows the names of parents, their nationalities, and whether they are still living.

The problem with this *thabian baan* is that people sometimes forget or are not able to make proper entries. This happens when a family lives far from the district office and the mother of a new baby finds it inconvenient to go to make the new entry. The result is often that a child's birth is not registered at the proper time and, rather than pay a fine for a late entry, the child's mother may simply skip the trip and wait until another baby is born. Then she may register the first child—but with a more current date of birth, though it is wrong. As a result, many Thais do not know their true birth date and are not sure of their age. This leads to mild confusion when it comes to registration for military conscription or admission to school.

Most Thais know the day of the week, and even the time of day, they were born. Horoscopes and fortune-telling depend upon the day of the week and the exact time you were born. Thais think it remarkable that *farangs* know the date of their birth, but not what day of the week or time it occurred.

Tourists and ordinary expats, of course, are not eligible for a *thabian baan*. Usually a copy of your passport is accepted in lieu of a household registration. In fact, just as all Thais are required to carry their ID card on their person at all times, so tourists are expected to carry their passports at all times, for the same reason. This is not always practical and safe for the visitor, so a photocopy of the relevant personal and visa pages should suffice until it becomes necessary for you to produce your actual passport for whatever reason.

Resident foreigners, those who have been accorded permanent resident status, must be on the household registration at their home

address and must change it if they move, just like a Thai citizen. Resident foreigners are not eligible to have a *bat prachachon* but are supposed to carry their 'alien book' (*samot tang dao*) and their 'residence permit' (*bai samkhan thin thi*). The *tang dao* must be renewed every year through your local police station, though it can be done at five-year intervals, depending on your agreement with the police station. The current cost of an extension should be checked at the Immigration Department (call 1111 for the hotline on government services).

For a long time, I was registered in Bangkok Noi district and went to the police station there to pay my extension fees every five years. On one occasion there was an old Chinese matron sitting on a bench in the office. She saw the policeman collect 800 baht from me and started to cackle. She said, in Chinese, "How come he has to pay 800 baht when I only have to pay 200 baht? Why does he have to pay so much?"

The officer pointed at the signs on the wall in English, Thai, and Chinese that there was a reduction for paying ahead: 800 baht for five years instead of 200 baht a year. She couldn't read the sign and had been paying 200 baht a year for perhaps forty years. And she was incensed that I was getting a reduction she had never known about. I can still hear her yowls of outraged Chinese.

Depending upon the circumstances, a death certificate must be acquired when an expat or tourist dies. This is issued by the Royal Thai Police and must be registered with the embassy or consulate of the deceased's home country. When an older person dies (say, someone aged sixty and up) the police may regard it as a natural death of old age; but when younger people die, a police investigation may be required before a certificate of any sort will be issued.

The government issues marriage and divorce certificates, the latter only if the former has been issued. Couples in an unregistered marriage (more than half of all marriages are not registered with the district office) will not be granted a divorce certificate. Some expats who married a Thai citizen abroad must re-marry here to qualify for a divorce. This is most often done because of complications dealing with citizenship, immigration, and land ownership.

While Thai law on acquisition of citizenship is revised from time to time, you should know that a person born in Thailand does not automatically hold Thai citizenship. The law states that the person's father must be a Thai in order to qualify. In other words, it's not where you are born, but to whom. This differs from the US and some other countries where you are entitled to the citizenship of the country in which you are born.

As for dual citizenship, it is best to consult a lawyer or a consular official with experience in these areas.

Any conscription-age young man with Thai-*farang* parentage had best check out his status, too. It is possible he has been naturalized in one country, but has not lost his original citizenship. Thus he may be required to abide by the laws on military service in both countries without even knowing it.

In almost all of these more complex issues, it is best to consult a lawyer or a consular officer. Among foreign visitors, a few free souls just ignore the whole matter, letting their passport and visas expire, not properly registering with the police, using assumed names, and, in general, thumbing their noses at the plethora of official paperwork. These people, when caught, may spend time at a Thai government 'resort' with iron-barred windows, at government expense, before being fined and deported elsewhere. Overstaying your visa results in a fine charged per day, and possibly jail and expulsion from the kingdom—at your expense. It's better to keep your affairs up to date and in order, don't you think?

Thailand has fierce anti-drug legislation on the law books, though it is only recently that is has been enforced as resolutely as in Malaysia and Singapore, with their mandatory executions for possessing more than a few grams of heroin. Thailand now hands down execution sentences or jails traffickers for life terms for possession of heroin or the methamphetamine known in Thailand as *yaa baa*. And an annually rising number of foreigners languish in jails for unwise possession, use, or transport of prohibited substances.

Compulsory Military Service

Although the military appears to be using it less and less as a source of bodies to staff its brigades and regiments, there is military conscription in Thailand. Every April, all 21-year-old males must assemble in their home districts, where they're given a physical exam and a chance to 'win' a black or red token in a lottery. Black means 'go back home.' Red, however, means 'you're in!' He has been drafted for two years' service. The lucky youth then waits for orders to report to this or that camp or military installation.

Thai men who want to enter the services can volunteer without taking part in the lottery system. Upcountry, men are more amenable to being recruits than are most city men.

Some young men buy their way out of the military lottery with what is an open and direct bribe. The amount varies from year to year, according to how many recruits are needed. While illegal, it also seems institutionalized. The other services may draw from the conscription pool, as well, if necessary. Navy recruits ordinarily come from provinces on the Gulf or Andaman Sea coasts.

Which Came First, *Kai or Khai*?
Thai Language and Arts

Thai Language

Which Scotsman said of English, 'I cannae get ma tongue aroond the stoof?' Probably many Scots, and Frenchmen, Irish, Spaniards, and even a few Thais may have expressed the same sentiment. Still, that should be no excuse for expats not to try learning the national language. Any degree of fluency is better than none at all. "No time to study," the expat cries.

"Make time!" is the answer—but unfortunately, often not heeded.

The system of tones in Thai is often the bugaboo monster that terrifies Western should-be learners. The five famous tones leave many paralyzed with fear, unable to open their mouths without dreading to think what other people might be hearing. They're not being unreasonable. They may truly feel inadequate to the tasks of differentiating their doctor from a cooking pot, or a horse from a dog:

doctor (*moh*) หมอ
cooking (*moh*) หม้อ
dog (*ma*) หมา
horse   (*ma*) ม้า
rice (*khao*) ข้าว
white (*khao*) ขาว

Of course, some listeners might take offence, but, generally, Thais will delight in this kind of error and then ask you to repeat after them some word or phrase that they know is a tongue-twister for expats. Still, getting your Thai friends and colleagues to help you is truly worth the effort. (And if you move fast, you can enjoy their help before they can get you to help them with their English!)

A standard Thai tongue-twister is the short sentence, *Kh(r)ai khaai khai kai*? 'Who sells eggs chicken?' Or, 'Who sells chicken eggs?' You

will step into the mire of trying to distinguish *k* for *kh*, while at the same time not forgetting the often silent *r* in *kh(r)ai* and the duration of the *ai* vowels, let alone the tones. You'll doubtless make a fool of yourself sometimes. Everyone will laugh with you. So, like the good sport you are, join in the general hilarity and have a good laugh, too.

Carlos' Language Lesson

Carlos arrived in Thailand with a fierce determination to immediately master the language, get himself a Thai wife, and settle down. And he did . . . almost. Within a few months he could speak intelligibly, but not very intelligently. He learned the language he needed at the markets, but not much else. For a wife, he found a girl from the Northeast (Isaan), whose Thai was accented and whose vocabulary was rich in colloquial terms. She became what was once called a *mia chao*, a 'hired wife.' We called her Carlos' wife, and everyone was happy with the arrangement.

One day Carlos' wife asked Carlos to go shopping for fruit. There may have been a few other items on her list, but bananas was what he planned to search for first at the crowded little outdoor market where the National Library now stands. Feeling very Thai, Carlos set out for the market, basket hung over his forearm. It's not so unusual for Thai men to do the shopping, so no one paid much attention to him as he stepped off the footpath into the unpaved market area. Sitting on tables amidst their piles of fruit and vegetables, purple shrimp paste, eggs in plastic sacks, banana leaves for wrapping, and rusty scales for weighing, were the vendors. Almost all of them were women. They chatted noisily and scarcely could be understood for the wads of *maak* (the betel leaf and areca nut concoction) that filled their mouths.

Carlos studied a pile of bananas and found them rather small. The vendor, a fat and very loud woman, looked at him and asked, "*Tongkaan alai kha, khun?*"

Challenged with a direct question, Carlos understood. "What do you want, you?" Carlos practiced his riposte a bit to himself, then bravely uttered a counter question, "*Khun mi khuei yai, mai?*"

The vendor gasped, came close to swallowing her wad of *maak*, and shouted loudly enough for the entire market to hear: "You want to know what this one asked me?" And of course everyone did, including Carlos, who did not understand her reaction of shock and wild humour. "He asked me if I had a *khuei yai*! Me!"

51

Her laugher came as a shrill scream, like a siren from a fire truck, but louder and clearer. Her tears ran rivulets down her facial wrinkles, and her belly bounced like the fields around Pompei during that historic eruption. Everyone else began screaming and laughing and passing the word until the whole market echoed with laugher.

Poor Carlos knew then what he had asked the vendor. He was so embarrassed it was all he could do to flee without upsetting the merchandise.

What was it that he said that was so awful? Well, remember those deadly Thai tones? Now let me remind you that local people often drop the *l* and *r*, or switch them around. Instead of asking the woman banana seller if she had any 'big bananas' (*kluai yai*), he had enquired if she had a *khuei yai*—a 'big penis.' It's exactly the sort of humour that sets some Thais laughing. But remember one thing: if Carlos had gotten his nerve up to go back to that market, he would have been remembered fondly and with good humour as one who had helped to brighten everybody's day. They wouldn't have thought that Carlos should be so embarrassed.

Give It a Try

Instead of deciding that Thai may be impossible to learn, or English just as difficult to teach, give it a whirl. You might, unlike my old friend Carlos, learn some of the basics of social conversation and have some fun doing it. If you give yourself a chance with a positive attitude, you will probably be able to learn enough to make everyone think you really *phut Thai keng keng*—'speak Thai very well.'

At one time, the Thai and Chinese languages showed many similarities. Still today they share certain qualities: both have tones, for example. Thai was also modified by later wholesale importation of vocabulary from two ancient Indian languages, Sanskrit and Pali. These carried a specialized vocabulary of religious, philosophical, scientific, geographic, medical, legal, and governmental terms into Thai, and provided the written alphabet. Thai is not written with characters, ideographs, or pictographs, but uses an Indian-based alphabet written from left to right, the same as all European languages.

Think for a moment of the role of Greek and Latin in English. Latin gave us our written alphabet, closely related to Greek from which it derived. In the case of Thai, you can compare Sanskrit as the equivalent of Greek in English, and Pali as the later Latin root.

Both Sanskrit and Pali are polysyllabic, non-tonal languages with inflections such as plurals and genders, tenses, and complex grammar, of which Thai has little. In this respect, Thai is much less complicated than German, Russian, or any other European language. The grammar resembles English in its basic subject-verb-object form.

You as a student of Thai will not have to memorize long lists of verb forms or irregular verbs, nor the irregularities of nominative, genitive, accusative, or dative variations on a noun, pronoun, or adjective. Most native English speakers don't remember these very well from their school days anyway. Unlike German, for example, Thai has no complex variations of the word 'the' (*der*, *die*, *das*) and nine other forms. You can be grateful for the easy grammar in Thai.

Having graduated from *prathom* four (equivalent to American fourth grade)—at that time the level required for foreigners to teach in Thai schools—I have passed through the fire of learning Thai, though my pronunciation leaves a lot to be desired. So I can say that studying Thai should hold no terror for a Western student. It's the tonal system that buffaloes almost everyone, and stops most would-be learners from jumping in and having fun.

One project that might make studying Thai less mysterious is to discover how many Thai words are linked to English, often by an ancient cord between German, Latin, Greek, Farsi (Persian), or Sanskrit. For example, 'cow' in English is the German *kuh* and *kho* in Thai. And 'brother' is German's *bruder*, and in Thai a rather classical *bharadar*, as in *bharadaraphap*, or 'fraternity.' As a fancy word for brother, it is pronounced *bharadon* and is sometimes used as a man's name.

With a little imagination, you'll soon be discovering many words in Thai that you have known for years, not to mention all the modern borrowings like *baengk*, *brek*, *and bia*, or 'bank,' 'brake,' and 'beer.'

Keep in mind that most Thais will welcome and appreciate your willingness to make an effort. Once in a while, you may run into some harassed individual who won't appreciate your attempts. He or she may be busy or tired of trying to understand some mumbling foreigner who is mangling Thai, but that person will be an exception. If you do manage to get out three words in a row that make sense, people will oooh and aaah and tell you how well you speak. You know that you don't speak much at all, but take it as a compliment anyhow. Smile and say, "*Khop khun maak*" ('Thank you very much').

Tones

It is true that the Thai language has five tones—even, low, falling, rising, and high—and that any 'word' pronounced in a selection of these tones is a different 'word.' There may even be a sixth tone, according to some dictionary makers. (Frankly, I don't know what the sixth is supposed to be, and find five absolutely enough to cope with.) And, to make things more difficult for the student, if you cannot read Thai (where the tone is clearly marked), the Roman alphabet does not lend itself to indicating vowel length or the tones without getting into tortured re-spellings:

ma—หมา;

ma—ม้า;

ma—มา

These words do not mean you need your mother. The first *ma* is spoken in a rising tone, like *ma?* and means 'dog.' The second *ma* is spoken in a high strangled tone and means 'horse.' The third *ma* in a neutral, non-rising and non-falling tone means 'come' as in 'come here.' (Are you still with me, or have you asked for a transfer to Bulgaria?)

So there are words where tone is important in defining meaning. But not all Thai words use tones. King Rama VI (Vajiravudh), who spoke and wrote English well enough to translate Shakespeare's plays into Thai, once explained that only in a few single-syllable words is the correct fixed tone utterly necessary for comprehension. In words like *witthayu* ('radio'), *torasap* ('telephone') or any other word of several syllables, it would be difficult to confuse it with any other.

His late Majesty suggested that students of Thai not panic. Just learn the correct tones on the dozen or so key single-syllable words that cannot be understood correctly if imperfectly pronounced "since the context would always make clear the meaning" in the rest of the entire language. Now that's not as bad as you thought, is it? This is true even if His Majesty may have oversimplified the situation a bit. If we're talking about herding animals it would make a great difference whether one was speaking about *ma* 'dogs' or *ma* 'horses.' It also makes quite a difference, I have found, if one says *muu baan* ('village') or *muu baan,* meaning 'a pig kept as a house pet.'

Practice with Thai speakers until you hear and say things correctly, so you won't confuse 'dogs-horses-come.' If you don't keep your Thai friends busy helping you with your pronunciation of Thai, they'll be busy getting you to help them with their English.

Thai Writing vs. Romanization

Most teachers of Thai and writers of Thai-language training manuals appear to think expat students of Thai are dumbbells and cannot possibly learn to read Thai letters. It's not as easy as our ABCs, of course, but written Thai is learnable and fun. You can learn a lot about the language if you can read, however slowly and haltingly.

The Romanization systems, of which there are almost as many as there are teachers, can be very confusing and misleading. Every writer has invented his own favourite concoction of letters aimed to convert Thai language sounds into Roman script, and what a mess has resulted.

The *Bangkok Post*, for example, writes *klong* for 'canal,' and they're right that this is close to what the Thai word would look like if they said

'canal' in Thai. A problem arises in that *k* in the government-promoted Romanization is a sound much closer to the first *g* in 'gong.' The *k* sound is indicated by writing *kh*. So *khlong* it used to be until expats decided that *kh* should be *k*.

No harm done, you may say. We say '*klong*' right, don't we?"

Not so. This is more than a mere disagreement between purists and pragmatists. It you don't know much about orthography or the alphabetic system (adapted from Sanskrit), *khlong* if written as *klong* could well be a type of tall drum, a camera, a box, and possibly other meanings, as well. Here, look at this: 'orthawgraffee,' 'alfabettickle,' and 'scisstem' would pretty much get the English sound across, but prove misleading to a student of English. But then, English is far less 'fonetick' than Thai is in writing. With very few exceptions, written Thai indicates the exact sound of a word and its proper tone. That's why they have more letters in their alphabet.

You can learn to write, and then you're able to ask Thais to write down for you a new word you've just heard. When you get home, you can look it up in a standard Thai-English dictionary. People who depend on Romanization cannot do that.

The two basic and, in my opinion, best systems for Romanizing Thai are that of King Rama VI and that of the Royal Institute, and neither is perfect. The King Rama VI system ultimately originates from work the British did in India in the nineteenth century. This system had been created so that British administrators, with only a modicum of instruction, could read and write Indian words without necessarily having an intimate knowledge of the many Indian alphabets. Since the Thai alphabet derives from India, King Rama VI adopted this system, and it works between Indian and Thai words with Indian roots. An example might be *mahâraja*.

However, about fifty years ago, there arose a demand from Thais not classically educated in Sanskrit and Pali to invent a Romanization that more closely followed modern Thai pronunciation. This resulted in *mahâraja* being changed to *mahârat* or even later to *mahâratcha*, with no damage done to the Thai language. Lots of changes then appeared. Look, for example, at some place names: Nagara Rajsima became Rajasima and Ratcha Seema. Bejrapuri became Phetchaburi and Petburi.

Eventually spelling became chaotic and unsettled, opening the way for everyone to 'spell it like it sounds.' Like it sounds to themselves, that is. This led to incredible confusion in newspapers and magazines, particularly in the matter of names. Because of the misuse of the system, you might not even recognize your best friend's name in print.

A Teacher's Tale

Once upon a time I was a teacher of Thai to students of an international school here in Bangkok. There were Indians, Americans, Japanese,

Scandinavians, Khmers, Vietnamese, and some Jews from various countries in my class.

I found the Indians (who usually could speak fluent Thai) were almost incapable of learning to read and write Thai. This was primarily because they were illiterate in Hindi, or any of the other languages that shared their writing with Thais. The Americans were a mixed bag—some learned well and some never conquered the idea of an unfamiliar alphabet at all.

The Jews who had studied Hebrew, and the Japanese, did very well. They were already literate in their languages and could pick up Thai as simply one more set of rules and characters.

Most amusing to me was an American boy who spoke current and slangy Thai, but in the eight months of our school year together seemed unable to learn to write a single word of it. He was, despite his verbal fluency, well on the way to earning an F in written Thai.

Then, one bright day, my teaching assistant showed this boy how to write a curse word in Thai. The American boy practiced the characters by means of rote memorization, repeated over and over again. Suddenly the light flashed. He had discovered the key to writing Thai, and write he did—all over his schoolbooks, his notebooks, the classroom curtains (in felt pen), in the dust on the sides of school buses, on washroom doors. He wrote and wrote his curse word, and his non-Thai-reading teachers never caught on.

Nor did his parents, nor the parents of his friends who couldn't read his scratching on their children's books and notes. But their domestic staff could, and they raised holy hell. But by then our hero was well on his way to a larger vocabulary and passing the course with flying colours. His ability, once unleashed, was extraordinary, and in the end he earned an A, the only one in his entire school career.

A Word of Warning

In the beginning stages of learning Thai, you will routinely pick up phrases that are inaccurate for you to use, or even impolite slang. This can happen to anybody, without even knowing it. Trying to copy Thai people's language leaves you in danger of picking up some unsuitable uses of Thai.

It was amusing to hear some burly, all-macho American sergeant during the Vietnam War say *sawatdi* ('hello' and 'goodbye') and then tack on *kha*, the polite particle used by women and some effeminate male homosexuals. It made a confusing—and amusing—picture for many Thai people. A man is supposed to add *khrap* to his phrases, pronounced more like 'cap' than 'crap,' please.

Thais sometimes impose their linguistic patterns on the English as they know it. The use of the Thai *kha* and *khrap* is relative to the sex of the *speaker*, whereas the English 'sir' and 'madam' go with the sex of the one *spoken to*. This can lead to some amusing contradictions, such as when a Thai man addresses an expat woman as 'sir.' The speaker is merely translating his *khrap* and using the particle for himself, rather than for the person he is speaking to. Perhaps even more startling is when a Thai woman addresses her expat boss as 'ma'am' under the impression that is the proper translation of her *kha*.

The word that is always proper to use for 'you' for people you're trying to be polite to—but not children, maids, drivers, and gardeners—is *khun* (pronounced like 'coon' but with the vowel sound very short, as in the English 'put' [not as in 'racoon']).

Sarongs, Bread, Beer, and Boutiques

Look at these foreign additions to the Thai language: *sarong*, Malay for a man's wrap-around-the-hips garment; *pang*, a Thai mis-hearing of the Portuguese *pão* or 'bread'; *bia*, Thai for the German or English 'beer'; *butik*, Thai for the French import 'boutique.'

Even Arabic, Farsi, Spanish, Vietnamese, and, above all, Khmer have added their spice. In fact, for reasons of historical closeness, Khmer and Thai share about fifty percent of their vocabularies, and Lao shares even more with Thai. Lao has more in common with Thai in general than the Southern Thai dialect has with Central Thai.

Ready to Start?

Before you plunge in, there are several ways to study Thai. One problem is solved for you just by being here: local assistants abound. The only snag could be that your maid or driver is Lao, or from Isaan where Lao is the base language, or from one of the Khmer-speaking provinces of the lower Northeast, and may not have a deep knowledge of Thai or even pronounce it right.

Get yourself a good dictionary, one large enough so that you can read the print without having to use a magnifying glass. The small, pocket-type dictionaries are easy to carry but nearly useless for a learner because they leave out too much. For a test, look up the entries for 'get,' 'set,' and 'mind.' These are English words that share several meanings, such as: 'get up,' 'get out,' 'get on,' 'get in,' 'get on with it,' 'get it over with,' or 'get set.' And 'set' could mean 'set' the table or 'set' the foresail. There is cement 'setting' as it dries, stage 'sets,' 'sets' of dishes, or 'set' in your ways. As for 'mind,' there is 'mind' your own business, a 'mindset,' 'mind your head,' 'mind your manners,' lost your 'mind,' or a 'mind' of her own.

See what I mean? A good dictionary is one that will make all these distinctions. It will be too heavy to lug about, or it may be in two or more volumes, so keep it at home and work with it at your desk at a particular and regular time every day, say for an hour. You'll begin to learn slowly, and, later, quite explosively. First you'll learn enough to get around, then to bargain, and finally to make friends and exchange ideas. When you reach the point of understanding jokes and word play, you'll find life in Thailand a whole lot richer. Certainly more so than those poor folk who never learn more than a few misused and mispronounced nouns and can't read a single word.

Stages of Learning

The experts say that there are two stages in learning Thai. The first is when you know some words, pronounce them with a passing fluency, and your Thai listeners assume that you know a lot more than you really do. They'll babble on at you, leaving you feeling like a beached whale, unable to employ the few words that you do know. Then you'll revert to English or sign language or simply try to get away with a nod and a smile.

The second stage will be when you understand a lot more of what's said than you can say on your own. Or, you're able to hear the proper pronunciation in your head but are unable to get it out of your mouth. That's the way with me and horses: I can hear in my mind the correct way to say 'horse,' but Thais who are listening to me are confused because they hear 'dog' all the time.

At home, I ask my son Bancha to bring me down a white shirt. He balks. "We have no white tigers upstairs."

"Who said anything about tigers?" Then I realize that I've erred in pronunciation. I think I am saying the word 'shirt,' but he is hearing the word 'tiger.'

Here are some different ways of studying Thai and my personal recommendations about them:

Try learning on your own, with books and tapes. Ughh! If you like studying alone at your desk at 5:00 a.m. or again at 11:00 p.m., I suppose this is fine. If you're a more social animal, then it may prove pretty dry, as there's no chance for interaction or questions.

In class. You can waste a lot of time getting to class and back, and if there are a lot of students, you may not get more than a minute or two of the teacher's attention in any one session. Except for the social aspect, I'd say this is not very effective, though a talented teacher may be able to keep everyone awake and learning. But beware that some teachers here aren't very well trained, so always enquire about the person's credentials and experience.

Form a class of your own amongst colleagues or family, and then engage a well-referenced teacher. This can be fun if people will attend regularly. Pressures of work or social engagements might sabotage this arrangement.

Private tutors will come to you (their time in traffic), or you will go to them (your time in traffic). Either way, it's better than a class that you get lost in. You tend to do your homework more if you're the only student.

If it can be arranged (and it is probably not easily done), live and work with Thais. Spending as much time as possible in Thai-speaking environments logically produces a better understanding of the language. This is called the immersion method. I think of it as being thrown into the pool at the deep end first. You either sink or learn to swim.

This last method is what helped me with my fragile French. I managed to get a job aboard a personal yacht as a deckhand and spent a whole summer sailing about the Mediterranean with a French captain and crew that didn't speak any English. Before I finally signed off the pretty yacht *Fingal*, I spoke passable late-eighteenth-century maritime French.

Be careful that this isn't the type of Thai you learn. But if you do, at least try to enjoy being the object of hearty laughter, all in good fun.

Thai Literature

Do you think you can learn about a people from perusing their national literature for heroes, heroines, the good guys and gals of their national mythology? And the villains? Can they tell us anything at all about national attitudes? I think they can, and here's why: Don't many Americans relish Jesse James' antics—robbing trains and banks with a bit of bloody slaughter thrown in for colour? Supposedly, he was also a bit of a Robin Hood, as it is said he stole from Northern US citizens to give back to his defeated Confederate comrades after the American Civil

War. Jesse died from a traitor's bullet, appropriate to his lifestyle, and so garnered much public admiration. In fact, there is so much interest still in Jesse James, that when the story of his death was doubted, his grave was opened in 1995.

Let's look at some of the more popular tales of the Thais and see if we can learn anything about Thai values and culture from them.

Hanuman, the White Monkey

Going back into prehistoric India, from which much of Siam's early culture and language originate, we find a famous story called *The Ramayana*. In a version first written in the third century BC and later revised by King Rama II, it is known in Thailand as *The Ramakien*. It is a story constantly re-mounted in productions on stage, film, and television.

The Ramakien is a tale of love, betrayal, and war. It tells of the conflict between good and evil, as do many American 'horse operas' with their good guys in the white hats and the villains in black. So in *The Ramakien*, the good guys are gods and princes supported by monkeys, and the bad guys are demons, giants, and their allies.

The main good guy is Prince Rama of Ayodhya (a city in India) who has been cheated of his inheritance by conniving relatives, driven into the forest and much mistreated by Ravana, the demon king of Lanka (Sri Lanka). Ravana kidnaps Rama's fiancée, Lady Sita, and whisks her off to his lair with no good intent.

Prince Rama has to fight the demon king and his evil armies to get her back, and calls upon a monkey band to help. The monkeys' general is Hanuman, white and agile, and rather tricky to boot. Hanuman and his simian corps come to Rama's aid and manage to rout the demon king's forces and free Lady Sita to return to her banished prince. In the end, Rama and Sita return to Ayodhya where they are greeted by an overjoyed populace. Rama is restored to his rights and becomes king.

This is the simplest explanation of this 147-act play. Due to its length, only bits and pieces are ever performed at one sitting. In Thailand, the last scene showing the death of Ravana the demon king is not acted at all. That part is considered very unlucky to show, but the public loves the many other episodes. Thais can tell you who among the many characters is related to whom, and what they represent.

Prince Rama is the honest man and the demon king represents badness in all its excesses. However, it is Hanuman who gains the public's admiration. What does he do to deserve this?

The demon king allows Hanuman to join the Lankan side and to worm his way into the royal confidence, learn palace secrets, and, in a moment of misplaced trust, puts his soul in a glass jar and gives it to Hanuman to put in safekeeping. Hanuman, however, reveals it, leading Prince Rama to victory.

Hanuman, scratching and leaping about the stage, amuses the public with his antic cavortings as well as his sharp intelligence used to end the war in favour of the good guys. Bravo!

What do Thais get out of this story? One moral could be that being clever may require a bit of betrayal, but in the end this is a way one can win a war, or any contest for that matter. Thais have an accurate saying that 'in a battle between elephants, the ants get squashed.'

This is particularly enlightening in the context of a small country. Thailand has usually been the ant trying hard not to get squashed by the elephants, and has learned to survive in many creative ways. Beyond that, the average Thai may learn that mental agility, ability to dissemble, bravery, and a highly developed cleverness are necessary qualities in order to enjoy success or to survive in many of life's endeavours.

The International School, Bangkok, Thailand's oldest school for expat children, used the white monkey as its logo. This was not lost on Thais, some of whom tended to regard many American teenagers living here as tricky monkeys indeed!

Sri Thanonchai

An even greater scamp and more immediate for the Thais than the cast in *The Ramayana*, is Sri Thanonchai, a character in an ancient story shared, like *The Ramayana*, with other countries. There are several versions, one of the most popular from Isaan.

Sri Thanonchai was born to a prominent noble family on the same day as the crown prince of the story's kingdom. As was the custom in olden days, he was removed from his family to be raised in the palace as a foster brother to the prince. Later, when the king lay dying, he bade Sri Thanonchai and the crown prince to act toward each other as true brothers. The old king had probably never heard of sibling rivalry.

The new king went on to govern his kingdom while Sri Thanonchai involved himself in many unsavoury activities, often getting the better of his royal master. The king was indulgent and took these situations as funny. But once in a while he grew angry with Sri Thanonchai, even banishing him from the court from time to time.

One day, the king fell ill and everyone despaired of his recovery. A court astrologer cast the king's horoscope and reassured everyone that, while the king appeared desperately ill, the stars indicated he would not die yet. Sri Thanonchai demurred. He told the queen that a true prediction would show that the king would die on a day within the week. The terrified queen did everything she could to save her husband, making merit and giving alms to the poor, and in a short time the king recovered. Later, the king questioned his foster brother about the erroneous prediction.

"Not a mistake at all, my lord," explained Sri Thanonchai. "Like everyone else, you will indeed die on a day in the week and not one outside of the week."

Thais make great use of this story and others that make a play on words, such as telling lies.

"I have never told a lie," someone declares.

"Never?" demands the one spoken to. "You've *never* told a lie?"

"I have, indeed, never told one lie."

"You're right. You've never told one lie. You've told many!"

Khun Chang, Khun Phaen

Thailand is suffering from many social changes produced by the shift from being agriculturally based to becoming more industrialized and developed: factories going up almost everywhere, tourists trekking throughout the land, foreign influences—movies, satellite television, the spread of new ideas in education—all of these are contributing to confusion and anxiety amongst the Thais. One problem area is the rapidly changing attitudes about the relationship between men and women. 'Men are the front legs of the elephant. Women are the back legs.' This traditional Thai idea is being challenged by the increasing education and mobility of women. No longer confined to their houses to raise babies, cook, wash dishes, and launder clothes, Thai women today are beginning to reject their status as objects subject to the whims of men.

A novel that clearly shows the status of men and women in what some men call the 'good old days' is *Khun Chang, Khun Phaen*. The story involves two men of the title's name, one rich but bald, the other about the same age but poor and handsome. Both are after the same woman, Nang Wan Thong. Wan Thong's mother is quite sure which of

the men is the better catch for her daughter: the bald one with money, called Khun Chang. But Wan Thong leans toward Khun Phaen . . . and all hell breaks loose.

It's a long story and very detailed, but it seems most Thais know the basic situation in the book, and maybe also in real life. This is the pressure on a woman to marry well. That meant traditionally to marry wealth or power rather than make a love match. In a traditional situation, now to a great extent disappeared, the parents of the girl would choose the groom, often employing a *mae sue* ('go-between') to check things out and to arrange the bride's price and other details. On a much lesser scale, it's like making a treaty between states.

While this system remains intact in some places—at least the money part—today's women have a lot more say in who is to be the groom. There's still a way to get around parents' opposition and that is to *pha ni*, or 'elope.'

Many a Thai girl in the past has faced the problem of her parents pushing her toward one suitor while her heart pined for another. Without these tales, Thai television soap operas would have very little to play about. Often, too, these stories don't work out too well for the girl. Suicides, abandonment, or life-long depression and despair are their lot. Or, as in Wan Thong's case, execution at the king's command.

To get a good picture of the Thais' ideas on marriage, love affairs, *mia noi* ('minor wives'), family pressure, or the insidious situation of rich-playboy-loves-poor-but-loyal-girl, or even worse, of a rich and independent single career woman who tries to get a poor but sincere boy, all you have to do is learn enough Thai to follow the prime-time soap operas. They show in graphic detail how a society is changing right before our eyes.

Phanthai Norasingh

In a country as impressively royalist as Thailand, you can expect an enormous amount of literature about kings and their subjects' loyalty to them. In novels, plays, songs, and in schools, the Thais teach the ideal of loyalty. Some of these stories may be off-putting to foreigners who

are a lot further away in time from their own absolute rulers and whose ideas about loyalty are therefore a bit different, as well.

One of these is the true story of the court chamberlain who forbade anyone to go to the help of a drowning queen and her baby. There was a palace law that prohibited anyone (even a doctor) from touching the king's consort for any reason. When the queen's boat turned turtle and she and the baby were thrown into the river, the chamberlain was not absolved from his duty to allow no one to touch the queen, even to save her life and the baby. She and her baby drowned.

Another story is often used to illustrate loyalty to a king, even when the king didn't want it. This is the tale of helmsman Norasingh who, in the time of the Ayuddhayan kingdom, was guiding the king's barge along a narrow *khlong* and, in a matter of tricky navigation, slammed the bow of the royal barge into a tree.

The palace law spelled out death for any boatman who smashed up a royal vessel, even if no one died in the mishap. The helmsman presented himself before the king and knelt expecting a fatal sword blow.

The king refused to have Norasingh beheaded as the law required. "You have done nothing wrong," he said. "You have merely mis-navigated and hit a tree. No one was killed, no one was hurt, and the damage to the vessel is purely superficial."

But Norasingh wouldn't hear of not being beheaded. He insisted it was the king's duty to punish him for not doing his own duty well. The king argued with him but Norasingh pointed out that if he were not executed, loyalty and exactitude in carrying out duties to the king would slacken and the court structure would ultimately suffer.

And so it went, back and forth, this study of a king willing to overlook what was an accident but his subject demanding that the king honour his own laws for the future safety of the realm. And so the king eventually gave way and Norasingh was beheaded.

How do you feel about tales of trickery and deceit, of misguided love, of one's sacrifice to a rigid concept of duty? Before you dismiss them as antiquated values of a yesteryear that is evaporating before your eyes, think again.

These and other cautionary tales have guided Thai culture for centuries, giving this country resilience as well as the stability to endure to current times.

Thai Music

As in Thai language, politics, food, and dress, many foreign influences come to bear on Thai music, as well. In the days before recordings and films, music in Thailand was mostly a do-it-yourself affair. People played instruments of their own invention and sang songs they made up, mostly for fun. In the village, almost everyone could hop about to a rhythmic beat. This is the origin of folk dancing everywhere. One result here in Thailand was that each region of the kingdom had its own typical music and dance, and this has persisted.

In Isaan music there are various simple stringed instruments employed to produce sweet, melodic music. There are others to be struck or scraped, each giving off a gentle sound of wood on wood. Another type of music uses gongs of varied sizes, and therefore different pitches and timbres. Fiddles with various numbers of strings, each with a coconut shell as its resonance box, are still popular in certain parts of the country.

Enormously popular is guitar and drum music imported in style and manner directly from the US and Europe. Sometimes it is also based on modern Japanese or Chinese music. This kind of music includes jazz and rock and roll.

Another kind of music, often labelled by foreigners as 'classical Thai,' is really court music, and was never widely played or heard by the ordinary public. It was restricted to the nobility in their palaces. This parallels the contrast between European chamber music and the more popular music for the masses of the same era. Mozart, Haydn, and most famous composers and musicians had to earn their living by inventing refined music for the lords and ladies of their princely courts. Most of Mozart's music (except perhaps for his most popular operas) was seldom heard outside of concerts, balls, and other events to which the great unwashed were not invited. Thus, the classical music of Europe was not popular—that is, public music—until the advent of recordings allowed the common folk to hear it, too.

This is even truer of Thai classical music. The public was not invited. It is only in recent years that Thai classical music has had a wider public hearing, and many Thais don't really enjoy it. "It's too sleepy," is the comment I've most often heard.

But it is this music, or at least one branch of it, that has caught the attention of music lovers and musicologists abroad. That one branch is the *phinphaat* or *piphat*. This is music that is obviously related to several Southeast Asian cultures: Thai, Burmese, Mon, Javanese, and Balinese.

The orchestra consists mostly of gongs, xylophone-like instruments made of wood or iron, and a variety of drums. Rhythm is kept by the use of *ching*, small bell-like devices struck together to produce a high-pitched beat, and *chaap*, a form of cymbals, as well as small blocks of wood or sticks. The music is a melodious cascade of notes and can be played very loudly. In fact, it is best to hear *phinphaat* music in a true theatre or outdoors rather than in a hall.

The other type of orchestra used for Thai music consists mostly of stringed instruments: a *khim* ('zither'), which is struck; and a *jakhe*, which resembles its namesake the crocodile and is first cousin to a Japanese *koto*. The old traditional *saw* is also used. These are the fiddles with coconuts as resonators. Many expats dislike the scratchy-gratey sounds of the *saw*, but it is true, as Thai musicians point out, that this instrument is the one most capable of imitating the human voice or other sounds in nature.

"Such as the yowling of a scalded cat," insists one expat friend. He is the one who said to me, "When you come to like Thai music, you've been here too long."

One thing it may not have in common, however, is the scale. The Thai *phinphaat* music is based on a five-tone scale. When Western songs that are based on an eight-note scale are played on the *phinphaat*, they may sound strange and distorted, but are generally recognizable after a few measures. Most Thai musicians are quite proud that they don't read notes, and seem to think less of European musicians for not being able to play more by memory. They do not seem aware that the absence of a common and widely accepted system for writing music limits them to playing only the repertoire that they have laboriously memorized.

While schools in Thailand often teach Thai music or have clubs dedicated to it, it is good to remember that this was never the music of the masses, aside from the Mon *piphat* that is played for funerals.

Song

Marginally more popular than classical instrumental music is the old-style singing. Few expats ever come to terms with this. They don't understand the poetry being sung, and they don't understand or particularly like the singing technique. Thai music doesn't have Western music's divisions into soprano, alto, tenor, baritone, and bass. Nor can Thai singing be divided by type of music, such as the West's opera, Broadway, blues, jazz, rock and roll, and so on. Thai music tends to let the voice climb up or plunge down the range or go into different timbres. This sounds very discordant to Western ears. It sounds nasal, too, as many of the sustained notes are on an 'n' or 'm' rather than a vowel.

Besides these unusual techniques (from foreigners' experience), there is a poetic syllable that Thai singers and poets use a lot, one that is hard to render in the Roman alphabet. One writer puts it as 'errr-ee' without pronouncing the r's. That sounds strange to some Westerners, too.

Thai poetry does not rhyme at the ends of lines, but has a complex theory of internal rhyme. Once you find out how it works, it makes sense. But it is subtle, and often expats cannot find the pattern. Books and pamphlets about this, published by the Department of Fine Arts, are on sale in some museums or, on certain occasions, at Bangkok's National Theatre.

Thai Dance and Theatre

While living in Thailand you may be able to buy some books on Thai theatre and dance. Or, you may be invited to attend the *khon* at the

National Theatre, the Chalerm Krung Royal Theatre, or at certain restaurants. What you find in the restaurants are not real productions of Thai theatre's danced and masked drama. Rather, they are more like rehearsal materials to allow students and teachers of these arts a chance to make some pocket money.

A *khon* festival of masks takes place for three days every June in Loei province. It, like most of the annual festivals scattered throughout the provinces, is colourful and boisterous and really worth the effort it takes to attend.

Do, by all means, pay attention to the cultural listings in the newspapers for what's going on. Look for a good example of a full company doing some episodes from *The Ramayana* (*Ramakien*) at a theatre. But be sure to read up on it ahead of time. Like many *farangs* at the opera, you may not be able to follow the dialogue at all, as it is sung or chanted in archaic, stilted, or poetic Thai—but you can at least find out what's happening on the stage before you go.

Thais like to sing, and they are not shy or embarrassed about singing at a party or even in what an expat would regard as strange places, like a classroom. So, of course, Japanese karaoke has become a big hit here.

For some years I was a stage actor. One of the hardest jobs was to memorize lines. I used to sweat blood over that, right up to the rise of the opening-night curtain. I have no memory for song lyrics either, not even for Christmas carols or a national anthem. Once, I asked my Thai play-reading students if they thought they could manage in a day or two to memorize one of the key speeches in a play. The students sighed with collective relief.

"Why? Is a paragraph too much?" I asked them. "You have three days."

"No, sir," replied one student. "We thought you wanted us to memorize the whole play by tomorrow's class."

I believe they could have done it, too. Thais memorize very well.

Training For the Theatre

One of the more interesting places in Bangkok to visit, although it isn't easy to get a pass to, is the Academy of Dramatic Arts (*Natasin*) located in a former palace on the grounds of which stands the National

Theatre. It is an ordinary academic high school, but included is the curriculum for demons, monkeys, and the other characters of the *khon*; and for singers, musicians, and dancers for the other types of Thai high theatre, there is *lakhon nai*, *lakhon nok*, *likay*, and other performing arts.

Lakhon is a word for 'play' and can include *lakhon nai*—the inside-the-palace, all-female plays, (*nai* here means 'inside'); *lakhon nok*—outside-the-walls plays, often done by all-male casts, (*nok* here means 'outside'); and a type of play (*likay*) that today is much relegated to companies that are hired to play at funerals, fairs, and in market areas. Of course, today there is also *lakhon tee-wee*, or 'television plays.' There is a distinction between *lakhon phut* ('spoken plays') and *lakhon phleng* ('musical plays,' which might include opera).

It isn't meant as a compliment, but Western grand opera and Broadway musicals are sometimes categorized as *likay farang* because of the unrealistic action, such as the stagger-and-clutch one sometimes sees in opera or in parodies of opera. Western operatic singing isn't much more appreciated by Thais than classical Thai singing is by the average expat.

Just a word about another type of local theatre you might run into near bridges and in Chinese temples. This is commonly misnamed 'Peking opera' and is a rural cousin to it. In Thai it is called *ngiu*. Modern Sino-Thais generally cannot understand the dialogue, and many people find the techniques grating on the ear, particularly the enthusiastic use of gongs, cymbals, and drums. This form of theatre is slowly dying out.

Thai *nang yai* and *nang talung* plays presented by narrator and 'acted' by a buffalo-hide cut-out that is manipulated in silhouette against a white screen are also becoming rarer every year. In the south of Thailand there are still several all-night performances of the *nang talung*. An interesting feature of these performances, besides their going from dark till dawn, is that the dialogue of kings is often spoken in Sanskrit—which no one understands—but the ordinary characters use colloquial Thai, and often make contemporary allusions to local situations or politics.

Moh-Lam

This is normally associated with Isaan, and consists of programmes and competitions of poetic wise-cracks sung between men and women. The villagers relish the dialogue and its sharpness.

The Chandarakasem Teacher College in Bangkok occasionally puts on *moh-lam* performances in English for the benefit of foreign visitors to the campus. These are great fun, so watch for announcements of such performances.

Western-Style Spoken Plays

Stemming mainly from the universities (several of which have drama departments) is an irregular flow of contemporary plays. These may be presented at the universities or in halls tucked into high-rise buildings of insurance companies or banks, in addition to the recognized theatres, which are expensive to rent for rehearsals and performances because of air conditioning bills. There are a few real theatres, such as the ones at the American University Alumni Association language school (AUA), the Alliance Française, the British Council, and the Goethe Institut. Some of the large hotels also have a hall where plays and concerts can be performed.

Small struggling groups do manage to put on plays, mostly translations from Western playwrights' works, some 'acclimatized' to Thai ways and culture. These productions seldom draw a wide public viewing. This is partly because of high ticket prices and partly because the actors, unless they also appear on television, do not draw the public. But put a television romantic actor in the cast and the hall will fill! A serious play or a tragic drama will draw only connoisseurs.

The cleavage between 'classic' opera music and modern rock is the same between Thai classic music and its own rock music. It is generational and geographical. Thais are divided in their musical tastes between their modern folk or rock singers and the music they call *luuk thung*, which in English might translate as 'country music.' Few expats get into these scenes or are even aware of some of the performers who are sweeping the kingdom with their popularity. Certain Western performers are well known in Bangkok and other cities: Rod Stewart, Tina Turner, Michael and Janet Jackson, Madonna, Whitney Houston, and others of similar renown.

As you go about the country, notice the varieties of music and theatre available: classical and modern, Western and Thai in origin. What a feast for anyone willing to sit at the table.

Joss-Sticks and Salvation:
Religion and Superstitions

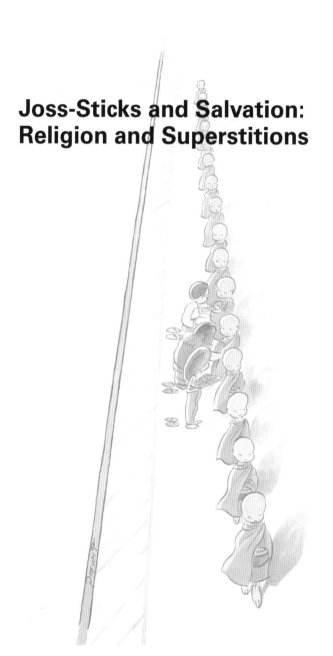

Buddhism

When you live in Thailand, don't be a slugabed. Arise early and go out on the street and you'll be able to see a sight seen in only a few countries: Buddhist monks on their food-gathering rounds—shaven-headed, barefoot men in orange-brown robes, each with a shoulder bag, carrying a metal bowl nestled in his arm. Perhaps a young helper will carry it, walking slowly through the still-quiet streets as the city or town wakes up. Faithful layfolk, men and women, will wait quietly by the roadside, and as a monk approaches they may slip into a respectful crouch, murmuring the Indian word *nimon* ('invitation').

The monk moves towards the one speaking, opening the lid to his bowl at the same time. The one making the offering holds up a plate or dish and very quietly spoons into the bowl whatever food or rice is offered.

The monk replaces his bowl lid and continues on his barefoot way, the layperson *wai*ing after him. In as many stops as it takes to fill his bowl and the upturned lid upon it (with fruit, tinned goods, or cartons of milk or juice being laid in the shoulder bag), his two meals of the day are thus secured. Lotus buds are often given, as well. The monk will then pad silently off to his home monastery. While most monks remain silent during this exercise, some may murmur a short prayer of blessing for the generous before moving on.

This act of *pindabat*, as it is called, has been repeated every day, in rain or sunshine, by Buddhist monks and laypeople for the past 2,500 years in South and Southeast Asia, as well as in the once Buddhist kingdoms of what are today India, Pakistan, Bangladesh, Afghanistan, Indonesia, Peninsular Malaysia, parts of China, Japan, Korea, Tibet, Nepal, Bhutan, Mongolia, and Central Asia. You may have read or heard about these Buddhist monks going out with begging bowls to gather their day's food, but that is not quite the way it is. Buddhist monks do not beg. Their duty is to offer laypeople the opportunity to practice *dâna* ('generosity') and to support their monks at the same time. The monks accept whatever is offered, and take the food back to their home, the monastery, where they can share it with whomever else lives there or eat in their rooms. They carefully discard foods that are forbidden to them. In times past this included human flesh, tiger, snake, horse, and others, the exact list varying from one Buddhist order to another. Chinese monks are vegetarians, but this is not a rule for monks everywhere. The Buddha himself, we are told, ate the food of the people he met. The Buddhist monk, even if not a vegetarian, may not consume the flesh of an animal he knows or believes has been killed especially for him.

In Southeast Asia there are several kinds of monks. Among the Thais there are two: *Mahânikaya* (the 'Greater Sect'), which covers the majority of the monks in Thailand, Laos, and Cambodia; and a smaller group called *Dhammayutikanikaya* that follows a slightly narrower interpretation of the monks' rules. In former times there was a third '*nikaya*,' the *Arannanikanikaya*, an order of forest-dwelling monks.

As for the monks who wear yellow trousers and a long-sleeved yellow jacket, they represent the ancient *Mahâyana* monks of the 'Greater Vehicle.' These are fewer than the *Theravadin* monks, the Thai orders who are followers of the oldest Buddhist disciplines. The *Mahâyana* are generally Chinese and are the only monks who may eat the supper meal. Unlike Thai monks, who may enter and leave and then re-enter the monkhood several times, the Chinese generally are monks for life. *Mahâyana* exists primarily in China, Japan, Korea, Nepal, Bhutan, Tibet, and Mongolia. *Theravadin* monks, sometimes called *Hinayana*, the 'Lesser Vehicle,' are today found in Thailand, Laos, Cambodia, parts of Southern China and Southern Vietnam, Burma, and Sri Lanka.

The *Mahâyana* is sometimes referred to as northern Buddhism, while the *Theravadin-Hinayana* forms the more conservative southern Buddhism. We can sum up these two great branches in an illustration: think of the northern branch of the Buddhist religion as a bus picking up passengers who want to ride to Salvation, the driver being a saviour figure. In this, you might say, northern Buddhism shares certain aspects that might be familiar to Christians, Jews, and Muslims.

The southern branch, on the other hand, is more do-it-yourself. Instead of a bus with a saviour-driver, you find a bicycle lying by the road. You feel like getting from A to B, so you get on the bike and, wobbly or not, you pedal yourself off to Salvation—on your own and without a personal saviour. What you do have is a map, the *Dhamma* (the 'Teaching'), wherein the Buddha explained the landmarks you'd come across as you pedalled along the road you decided to explore.

"A show-er of the way am I," the Buddha once said.

The destination in both branches of Buddhism is *nibbana* ('nirvana'), a state that we may experience, not a 'place' like 'heaven,' although many simple Buddhists may think of it that way. In this system, the cyclist may lay aside his bike, if he wishes, for another to pick up and use. The surprising thing is that the previous bike will still be there to carry you onward in life when you wish to return it.

Who Was the Buddha?

The man we call the Buddha (the 'Enlightened One') was Siddhatha Gotama, the son of an Indian raja. He was raised in the lush style of ancient royalty and was taught the martial arts. He was married, in the ancient arrangement, to his first cousin, and fathered a son. It would seem that he should have been the happiest of men.

This was not the case, however. At an early age he learned that life, taken as a whole, was not easy or pleasant. Birth is an unpleasant, even dangerous experience, being extruded from the protective, dark, and warm environment of a mother's womb into a hostile and frightening world. The account says that the Buddha's mother died when he was only a week old, and he was given to his aunt to raise.

As a protected and cosseted young prince, he had to study and learn archery and the handling of horses. Despite the best of everything his world could afford him, he also learned the darker themes in life: of ageing, working and striving, loss and uncertainty, sickness and death.

There is a fine chapter in the *Suttanta Pitaka*, the Buddhist equivalent of the Christian gospels, that tells of one of his excursions outside the palace walls. He and his charioteer galloped past a crowd gathered around a funeral pyre. He asked his driver what it was about, and the driver explained about death and how we all come to it.

During another excursion into the outside world of the city, he beheld a sick man creeping along the roadside, and on another occasion he saw an aged, crippled man, and so he learned about sickness and the infirmities of old age. 'Birth, age, sickness, and death.' These are four elements of life that the Buddha found productive of *dukkha*, a Pali word that included everything we find unsatisfactory—pain of a toothache, disappointment in love, a hangover, anything that is unsatisfactory. It is not the external thing that is *dukkha*, but rather our feeling about it.

On another outing from the palace, the young prince spied a man striding along energetically, apparently full of health and energy, his face radiating contentment. The prince asked, "Who is that man? What is he?"

The driver explained, "This man is a wanderer from home into homelessness, a mendicant religious." He explained that the man had found satisfactory answers to the prince's questions about life and was unbothered by the ills of birth, ageing, sickness, and the prospect of death.

This impressed Prince Siddhatha immensely. The idea of this *bhikkhu*—for that is what a religious wanderer is called in India—preyed upon the prince's thoughts until he, too, decided to leave home to seek the truth from teachers who could help him develop a more acceptable understanding of life for himself.

In a scene often repeated on Thai temple walls, you will see Siddhatha saying a quiet farewell to his sleeping wife and baby, escaping by night

from his palace, then riding his favourite horse to the river that marks the border of his father's realm. There he gives his heavy jewelled earrings to a companion, bids farewell to his horse (which is shown weeping bitter tears), and strides off into the unknown of the fearsome, dark woods. This popular scene is called the 'Great Renunciation.'

The story goes on about the now ex-prince's experience in seeking out teachers and recluses and philosophers, with whom he studied and practiced religious exercises. Indian religion of that day, 2,500 years ago, had two great divisions. Some practitioners sought out physical austerities to overcome the desires of the flesh, such as fasting and self-torment. This type of religious practice is still seen today all over India. Some call this the 'bed of nails' school of religion.

The ex-prince followed teachers from this school of thought until he was a mere bag of bones. Then he decided that this way only led to weakness, illness, and death. So he left them and moved to join those who practised the other great branch of Indian religion, the meditators. These are men and women who attempt to free their minds by long periods of turning their attention inward. Some call this the 'study of their navels' kind of religion.

The ex-prince practiced until he attained the same level as his teachers. He then said goodbye to them and left to carry on by himself. This bore fruit for him. Slowly, over many days and nights, there came to him what Buddhists call the 'Great Enlightenment.' This understanding about the true nature of life gradually became clear to him and became the basis of what he later organized, wrote, and taught across India for the rest of his long life.

What he taught is what we call Buddhism. The Buddha, as he became known, the Enlightened One, became a kind of living saint, showing Indians how to study their own minds and teaching them ways to make sure that their minds were calm so that insights into the universal truths arose on their own.

So, the Buddha was a renounced prince and heir to a small kingdom—husband, father, and son in an unimportant Indian principality—who became a wandering teacher promulgating a way of looking at life, and gathering around him a following of men at first and, later, women, who listened to his teaching and tried to practice it. *Buddha*, the Teacher. *Dhamma*, the Teaching. *Sangha*, the Taught. These are his followers then and today. Buddhists still call the men *bhikkhu*. In ancient times, when the women's order still existed, the nuns were called collectively, *bhikkhuni*.

When and Where Did All This Take Place?

Almost 26 centuries ago, in Northern India and what is today Nepal, Buddha's influence and the teachings he espoused spread all over Eastern and Central Asia, where it tended to become a religion for all. This had a distorting effect on the way the Buddha's teachings were carried out, so that today there are many practices in Buddhism that are rather more Indian, Khmer, Tibetan, Chinese, or Thai than in the original teaching he had left.

Where Can We Find His Teachings Set Out?

Buddhists have nothing quite equivalent to the Judaeo-Christian Bible. What replaces this source of authority for Christians and Jews is a record of the Buddha's life and activities, his teachings, and the rules he developed for his followers (the monks, basically, but also laymen and women), as well as a final section on the operations of the mind. These writings are collectively called "The Three Baskets," or *Suttanta Pitaka*, *Vinaya Pitaka*, and the *Abhidhamma Pitaka*. Not all of these have been translated into English, but the Thais have a full version in both Thai and Pali. Pali is, for Buddhists, as dead a language as the Latin of the Roman Catholic Church. But as with Greek and Latin in English, Pali has entered Thai in a flood of words and concepts, many of which are quite foreign to those (even Thais) not familiar with their Indian background.

Who Are the Monks Today?

Strictly defined, the monks—or *bhikkhu*—are men who meet a certain set of requirements and who have applied for membership—ordination—into the Order, the *Sangha*, which is the name for the Buddhist monastic family. They have been accepted for as long as they wish to stay, whether for life or only a short time. They dress in an easily identifiable way, and follow rules of conduct intended to free them from society's complicated demands.

What About the 'Nuns,' the Women in White Robes?

Technically, there may be both men and women in the white outfits. The women, for lack of a better word in English, are call 'nuns.' The Pali name *upasika* means 'extra-devout laywomen.' They seek freedom from life's demands by studying and practicing the Buddha's teachings, but they do not really represent an order of true Buddhist nuns. In Thai, these women are called *mae chi*, which is close to the English for 'nuns.' Only now are these devout women beginning to receive some of the respect they deserve.

There are also men in the white robes, called *upasaka* in Pali, though pronounced in Thai as *upasok*. Not so prevalent as *bhikkhu*, nor so honoured by society, an *upasaka* takes the state just below that of a monk, without encumbering himself with so many rules. A common nickname for them is *pho khaaw* ('white fathers').

The young boys who are not yet of age to qualify as full monks are called novices. In Thai this is pronounced *nane*, and they may be awaiting full ordination when they attain twenty years of age. There is no modern equivalent for young girls.

All monks, *mae chi*, *upasaka*, and *nane* are ordinary people of any age and background who have met the requirements to ask for ordination. These include being a human being, not being a slave or in debt, not suffering from boils or unsightly eczema, tuberculosis, or leprosy, nor disfigured with brands or sliced ears or noses (an old-time punishment for various infractions), nor anything else that might put off the laity, making it difficult for them to gather their food. You'll note that there are no professional requirements such as a seminary degree or other educational prerequisites such as those found in many Judaeo-Christian religions.

What Are the Rules for the Monks?

The thrust of all the rules drawn up during the Buddha's lifetime is to free monks to practice what the Buddha taught. There are 227 of these rules, varying from quite serious ones (violation of which will result in a monk's disrobing with no chance to be ordained again) to what appears to be etiquette to allow people of different backgrounds to live together peacefully.

The *Sangha* is a celibate order because the Buddha felt that unrestrained sexual activity produces many problems in society. Prostitution, rape, adultery, seduction, and other unacceptable sexual acts in general are forbidden to those undertaking the Buddha's training and will result in the violator's expulsion from the *Sangha*. While in the *Sangha*, a monk is forbidden sexual relations with men, women, animals, and ghosts. The Buddhist literature is very specific on all this. If a monk cannot uphold

celibacy, or any other aspect of communal monastic life, he is free to renounce it and to 'disrobe,' that is became a layperson again.

Other rules deal with relations to be maintained with laypeople, avoiding situations productive of lack of respect. Of course, the basic teachings must be upheld by the monks, such as a prohibition against killing other beings, stealing, drinking alcohol, using illegal drugs, or claiming special powers like fortune-telling. After all, if the Buddha's goal is for his followers to develop clear minds, then it makes sense that they may not use substances that produce heedlessness.

The monkhood requires a simple style of dress. As for one's hair, the Buddha recommended shaving it off once a moon and never letting it grow longer than three finger breadths. Buddhist monks today shave their heads and eyebrows fortnightly or on the day before the full moon. All of these rules have the intent of simplifying a *bhikkhu's* life while he is in the robes.

Some of the etiquette rules are amusing because we can relate to them two dozen centuries after they came about. For example, monks, while eating, should not make slurpy sounds nor put their fingers in the food bowls and then lap at their fingers. Nor should serious monks play silly games and pranks, such as playing practical jokes on other monks.

A new monk must remember the 227 rules to keep his practice correct. The Thai public is mostly familiar with the general tenor of these rules if not their specific contents and intent. For instance, Thais almost universally know that women must not touch a monk. What they may not realize is that this rule is addressed to monks, not so much to the laywomen. The rule actually says that a monk may not touch, caress, or cuddle a female with his mind misled by lust. Thai religious authorities, recognizing that observers cannot tell the state of the monk's mind at the time, have interpreted this rule as meaning, 'monks don't touch women and women don't touch monks.'

Women try not to make problems for monks by putting themselves into situations that could lead a monk (or the woman) to be criticized. If sexual contact is the fruit of heedlessness in avoiding these situations, the monk may be driven out of the *Sangha* altogether and the woman disgraced in the eyes of the public at large. Non-Thai women should recall at all times that monks cannot touch anything at the same time that the woman does. For example, a monk cannot give his bus ticket directly to a female ticket taker. He must give it to a man, who can then deliver it for him to the ticket taker. This is also why the last or first seats on buses are generally reserved for monks. It saves a lot of awkwardness for all concerned. In all events, a woman shouldn't be made to feel 'unclean' by this—it's simply to help the monk keep *his* mind off *her*.

Why, When Life As a Monk Is Narrowly Constricted, With So Many Prohibitions, Do Young Men Want to Become Monks At All?

Religious enthusiasm is often not the reason a young man enters the monkhood. Often, it is seen as a social obligation. If the son of a family is ordained, even for a short time, it shows the world that his parents have brought him up well. It showers the family with merit, a very Thai concept, which may help the ordinand's family to feel socially respected. They have raised the youth, and he has shown his gratitude by putting on the saffron robes for a period of time.

Also, some traditional parents cannot accept as a son-in-law a man who is not 'done.' He is not yet ripened in this society for not having been, even briefly, a *bhikkhu*.

Yet some men do seek admission to the *Sangha* when they find themselves in spiritually difficult situations. These include such seemingly bizarre reasons as being bedevilled by ghosts or bad luck, as well as a more easily understandable search for spiritual truth. They seek admission as a monk to study the Buddha's teaching more closely than can a layman with responsibilities to family and work.

To become a monk, Buddhists believe, is the best thing a man can do in this life, whatever his motivation. Becoming a monk is a way for an alcoholic, drug addict, or criminal attempt to reform. It can also be seen as trying to 'self-medicate' for depression, anxiety, and stress. Even His Majesty the king was a monk for a short while, as were most of his royal ancestors. King Rama IV (Mongkut) was a monk for 31 years before he acceded the throne.

I once knew a young Thai gangster who experienced a vision of what his activity might lead to. He joined the monkhood to try to prevent this from happening, struggling to straighten out the kinks in his life before he could be murdered by vengeful victims or caught, tried, and imprisoned by the authorities. What's the end of his story? The last I heard, he had found a true refuge and vocation in the monkhood and was still there.

Isn't the Buddha Often Considered God Or a God?

Some simple country people may think that but, as you have read, the Buddha was a teacher in ancient times whose teachings have been passed down to the present day. He certainly never represented himself as a god. One of the confusions about terminology is rooted in the Thai language. The term *phra chao* is often used by Thai Buddhists to mean 'lord.' It is, however, a word used by Christians and Muslims to refer to God, called Allah (the 'God') in Arabic. And it is used by Thais to refer to their king, to complicate things even further.

Phra by itself is an honorific that is used to refer to gods, noblemen, Buddha images, palaces, temples, monks, and even (Christian) priests, or anything else one wants to render special, sanctified, or holy.

As the Thai concept of god is Indian, and therefore multiple, it has been very difficult for missionaries of one-God-centred religions to get their points across. Christian missionaries of all denominations and sects have very few successes with conversions of Thai Buddhists. They appear to do better amongst Chinese and other non-Thai inhabitants of the kingdom. Buddhism is thoroughly established as the Thai religion, and so patriotism is often mixed with whatever theology is involved. Muslims are often denied the name 'Thai' by the general public due to this mix of nationalism and theology.

What Are the Basics of Buddhism?

Now, let's be sure we understand the basics of Buddhism as learned by the average Thai today. The truths Buddha considered central can be boiled down to four fundamentals, the Four Noble Truths:

All life is subject to unsatisfactoriness and unhappiness, which is termed *dukkha*. Birth is unsatisfactory. Growing old is unsatisfactory. Falling ill is unsatisfactory. The prospect of dying is unsatisfactory. While these are basic ideas, one can add many more, either serious and far-reaching or most mundane: being hungry or having gorged on too much food; war and disease; the development of a zit on a teenager's nose before a dance; being separated from what you like or love; being forced to be with what you dislike or hate; disappointment of all kinds. These and thousands more variables can be considered *dukkha*. Also remember that these things are not *dukkha* by themselves. The *dukkha* is your emotional reaction to these situations and your feelings when you encounter them.

The second truth is that all *dukkha* is produced by craving. You want to hear your concert without the flickering and buzzing on your television that a plane passing overhead can inflict. You're tired and you want to sleep peacefully but a group of inconsiderate motorcyclists' rendezvous under the street lamp opposite your bedroom. What can you do? Shout at them? You might reap a hail of rocks on your walls and roof. That would probably result in even more *dukkha* for you to deal with.

If you can accept your concert with the interference on the television, you might not experience the annoyance that would be *dukkha* in this situation. If you can just turn your thoughts away from your desire for sleep and accept the motorcyclists' interruption, you are not craving anything you don't have. You are not then, feeling *dukkha*. In other words, if you can eliminate your craving (for music, for silence), you experience no *dukkha* in these situations.

The third of the Buddha's Four Noble Truths is that by abandoning craving, you are then freed from *dukkha*. Too simply put, perhaps, but if you can accept the conditions of your life and the world, you will find that *dukkha* disappears.

Monks devote much of their time to studying this step in the process. It's the most difficult one so far, isn't it? If the Buddha had taught just this much, there would be little that is unique and original about it. Other religious teachers in India and elsewhere have come up with these ideas in one form or another. Where the Buddha's teaching differs from the rest is in the Fourth Noble Truth, the 'Eightfold Path,' which is a 'how-to' handbook for stopping craving and thus ending *dukkha*:

The Buddha devised his scheme of eight steps to be taken by his followers, both monks and laypeople. These require observation and study of one's own behaviour and making such changes as may be necessary to bring reform to one's life. These are described as the eight 'Rights.'

Right View. This is the knowledge that whatever your problem, the Buddha's teaching may offer a way out. Unlike in some other religions, this does not mean merely that you give assent to the teaching, but that you believe. Buddha didn't much credit belief all by itself, for the obvious reason that men have proved they can believe almost anything they want, without much real change for the better. '*Right View*' is merely the knowledge that the Buddha's *Dhamma* may hold something for your benefit.

Right Thought. The realization that your thoughts forerun and control your actions. Therefore, your thoughts must be examined for their wholesome and unwholesome qualities. The latter are productive of *dukkha*. The former may be put in a terser form: 'thoughts free from sensuous desire, ill-will, and cruelty.' To find out exactly what these are is sometimes not obvious and requires intense study.

Right Speech. The way we talk often reflects the way we think. In practical terms, it means to abstain from lying, tale-bearing, harsh language, and foolish babble.

Right Action. This means to abstain from killing, stealing, and unlawful sexual activities. 'Unlawful' here means abusive and exploitative rather than an absolute prohibition. Rape, of course, would be an example of abusive intercourse. Would prostitution be exploitative? Buddhists are studying this issue to determine what is wrong with these acts, why some are 'unlawful.' Or does the state of 'unlawful' reflect only the era and the jurisdiction? As the main character in *Teahouse of the August Moon* put it, "Pornography is a question of geography."

Right Livelihood. Many activities people engage in to earn their living may be productive of *dukkha*. Amongst these, Buddha included anything that brings harm to any other being, such as trading in arms, slavery, poisoning, slaughtering, fishing, soldiering, deceit, treachery, soothsaying (a big business in Thailand), trickery, and usury. Does the career of a butcher fall under this condemnation? If so, what can he do about it?

In the Buddha's time, a question arose when an officer of the king's forces came to him to enquire what he could do. He was a soldier and had to fight his king's enemies. He was uncomfortable with the fact that the exercise of his profession conflicted with his beliefs. The Buddha asked him, "Can you resign?"

"The king depends upon me. I cannot leave his service. It is my duty," the officer replied.

"Then do your duty," the Buddha advised. "But do not hate your king's enemies."

Right Effort. The effort of avoiding or overcoming evil and un-wholesome states within yourself, and of developing and maintaining wholesome states, also within yourself. To do this requires coming to know yourself very well, inside and out.

Right Mindfulness. A development of awareness, usually brought about through meditation.

Right Concentration. Meditative practices that are the gateway to further mental attainments.

One might say that, in Buddhism, meditation and mental develop-ment take much of the place that, in other religions, may be held by prayer, contemplation, and 'good works.' 'Petitionary prayer'—asking a god or saint for something, is useless in *Theravadin* Buddhism, as there is no god to pray to. Nevertheless, many Thais do 'pray' to the long-gone Buddha for help in their daily affairs. This is a popular misconception about Buddhism, as the Buddha's unique teaching to his disciples for their immediate benefit gradually evolved into a people's religion or, as it is today here in Thailand, a state religion. The king of Thailand must be a Buddhist as well as the protector of other religions in the kingdom.

There are many teachings attributed to the Buddha, but these few set out the basics. It may surprise you to find that Buddhism is not concerned with all the factors you may think of in the field of religion.

When and How Did the World Come Into Being? What About the Possibility of Being Reincarnated As a Millionaire Or a Cockroach?

On this last one, 'reincarnated' is not a Buddhist term. Buddhists use 'reborn.' It is not just a semantic difference. What Buddhism says on this subject is subtle and not easy to understand.

Buddhism has no glib catechism that gives the 'official' correct answers for Buddhists. In fact, the Buddha discouraged any line of questioning that was not conducive to his main goal, the elimination of *dukkha* for all people.

The Buddha would have asked this: Does knowledge of how the world came about make you any happier? 'Big bang' or 'leisurely accretion'—will either of these views of the primeval universe make you a better person, or will it merely titillate your intellectual sense unnecessarily?

As for being a millionaire or a cockroach in your next rebirth, that concept is Hindu or Brahmanistic, not Buddhist. However, if, say, you win the lottery, Thais will ask, "What did you do in your former life to deserve that?" The doctrine of rebirth can only be understood in terms of the Buddha's deeper teaching, and that requires considerable study to understand.

What Do the Monks Do All Day?

Many of them study, practice, meditate, write, read, preach, and give consultations. A few may also tell fortunes, play the horses, or repair television sets in their quarters. These latter types may be considered by devout Buddhists as wasting this wonderful opportunity—of being Thai, male, Buddhist, and a monk—to better themselves. But it still happens sometimes, the same way it does in all religions.

Why Don't the Monks Help With the Gardening in Their Monasteries?

Some non-Buddhists have observed that most of the yard work in *wats* is done by non-monks, very often by *mae chi*, the white-robed nuns.

The Buddha ordered monks to avoid anything that smacks of agriculture. There are two reasons for this: first, in the India of his day, the public was divided into castes. The top caste provided kings and warriors, and the Buddha, as a scion of the kings of his state, was one of these. The Brahmans (or Brahmins) were of the learned and teacher caste, a second level. The townsmen and merchant class formed the third caste. Below all of these castes and their many variants and subcastes stood the humble farmers and labourers who dirtied their hands in planting, harvesting, and other occupations. While the Buddha did not honour the traditional caste divisions in his world, he was aware that the public would be made quite uncomfortable if the lower castes were to live and eat with the upper ones.

The Buddha, as he often did, compromised on this issue. He would accept without discrimination members of any caste into the order of monks, even the Untouchables beloved by Gandhi later on. But he would not expect any of the monks to do agricultural work so that the public could not complain that upper-caste monks were doing low and degrading work.

A second reason is that agriculturalists kill animals and bugs. This violated the Buddha's rulings against his monks killing any living creatures. By forbidding this occupation to his monks he avoided public criticism and created internal theological consistency at the same time.

One must bear in mind that the monks receive their alms food from the laypeople, and their monasteries are supported by lay donations, and they form an honoured part of society. The Buddha wished to avoid any misbehaviour that might cause his monks to be criticized or scorned.

This is one reason why monks in Thailand are usually very careful about their behaviour. Though among some 100,000 men in an institution like the *Sangha* there are bound to be a few baddies, sometimes these are exposed, bringing sensationally awful press and defamation upon the Buddhist institution as a whole.

Can a Non-Thai Become a Monk?

If you're male and meet the requirements, you can indeed apply for ordination, whatever your nationality. There is no rule that you must be Thai or speak Thai, although you'll have to memorize the ordination service in Pali. The Buddha was of course not Thai, nor did he speak the language. But through translation, he spoke to the world of his time and ours.

What Do Buddhists Wish to Attain?

It would be too easy to say that Buddhists wish to attain some specified goal such as heaven or *nibbana* (an ineffable state or experience). Some may; some may not. And some don't understand the concepts at all.

To discuss what Buddhists 'want' would take a volume all by itself. However, there are four states that educated and practicing Buddhists do agree on as worthy of attainment. Here are the four states a devoted, practicing Buddhist aspires to:

Mettâ. This is loving kindness toward all other beings, including people you don't much like, animals, and insects of all sorts—including snakes, cockroaches, rats, and so on. Many Buddhists believe that if you can develop a feeling of loving kindness toward mosquitoes, they won't attack you for your blood anymore. As a monk, I experimented with this and found that, while some mosquitoes still may have bitten me, I seldom felt their bites.

Karunâ. Compassion toward all creatures. The Buddha was called in his lifetime the 'Compassionate One' because of his teaching and practice of this quality toward people, animals, and insects. His reasoning was that we creatures are all in the same existential boat—and it is leaking and about to sink. We all want to live, to find success and happiness and health; it behoves each of us as a sentient and thinking member of a universal society to act so as not to hurt other beings. In India, where these beliefs are also acted upon, you can find religions where the practitioners even cover their noses when they walk so as not to breathe in tiny creatures. Buddhists may not go so far as to carry brooms to brush the ground ahead of their steps so as not to crush creatures such as ants, but the Jains do. Devout Buddhists might press cloths to their water taps. This is not only to protect humans from ingesting the unseeable bugs in the water, but to protect the bugs from being ingested. One of the pieces of monk's gear that must be shown at an ordination is a water strainer to be used for the same purpose on taking water from a jar or tub.

Muditâ. This is the sympathetic joy you feel at another's success. For example, you and I decide to buy two lottery tickets. I add your money to mine and go off to buy the tickets. We split them, one for you and the other for me. On the day of the drawing it is announced that your number has won. Now, how do I feel?

With sympathetic joy, I must rejoice at your good fortune. If I growl and mutter, "I should have kept those numbers for myself," then I am not experiencing *muditâ*. Or, we're vying for the same promotion at work. The boss selects you for the job. How do I feel? Unfairly treated? Angry or envious? These are corrosive emotions, not sympathetic joy.

Upekkhâ. This is sometimes mis-translated as 'indifference.' It is rather the quality of equanimity, and it is directed toward yourself rather than outwardly onto others. You remain 'cool' to whatever happens to you. Think of the Buddhist teaching of *karma*, one of the Buddha's key teachings. If you experience pleasure or 'good,' you have brought it on yourself, so act calmly and accept it. On the other hand, if what comes to you is painful and ugly or 'bad,' accept that calmly, too. According to the Law of *Karma*, you deserve these by something you have done earlier, either in this life or a previous life. So, whatever happens to you, just accept it as coolly and calmly as a deserved reward for something you have done.

Loving kindness, compassion, and sympathetic joy are directed toward others; equanimity is directed toward yourself. These qualities—collectively called *Brahmavihare*, or 'Abodes of the Gods'—are virtues to be developed by Buddhists.

Why Are Buddhist Temples So Ornate?

Probably because that's the way the Thais like them and can afford them. Nevertheless, there are some new styles sneaking in quietly, as you will discover when you travel around the kingdom. Don't be shy about visiting a temple or even taking photographs. Just follow the usual Thai social rules about dressing modestly (no shorts or sleeveless tops),

removing your shoes in the chapel, and not sitting on the floor pointing your feet at the Buddha images or the monks. In some Northern Thai temples, there may be areas prohibited to women. But there will always be signs indicating this.

Most Thai holidays are connected with religion or the monarchy—'Coronation Day,' 'Dynasty Day,' royal birth- and death-days, and so on. The full-moon Buddhist holidays are Magha Puja, Visakha Puja, and Asalha Puja. These fall in January-February, May, and July, respectively, although the dates change yearly because they're set following the ancient lunar calendar of the Buddha's India.

Social Occasions: Ordinations, Funerals, and Weddings

One of the social situations expats find themselves confronted with may be an invitation from Thai friends or colleagues, or a maid or driver, to attend an ordination (*kaan buat*) or a funeral (*ngaan sob*). This often brings up questions of How do I react? What do I do? Must I go? How do I dress? What do I have to take or give?

The most prominent of the rites of passage in a Thai Buddhist man's life are his entry into the *Sangha*, his marriage and, at the end of his life, his funeral.

Ordinations

The importance of ordination is not based on how long the man is a monk, but instead on the fact that he became one. He may remain a monk for life, or, in certain special situations like the sudden death of a parent, he may be ordained for one single day. But in either case, he will go through the entire ordination ceremony and have his head shaved as any other candidate for the monkhood. He will be a full monk the entire time of his stay in the *Sangha*, even if in the evening of his ordination day he withdraws from the monkhood to return to his layman's life.

Friends and relatives love to attend an ordination ceremony, and anybody can go, whether or not the guest is known to the ordinand. Because

I was a foreigner and had enjoyed some publicity in the *Bangkok Post*, my own ordination into a small temple near Bangkok was attended by several hundred guests. Some were people I knew, like those I had worked with at the bank where I was teaching English, or at the university and various other schools where I had taught. And there were some I didn't know, but who gave me traditional gifts such as a ceremonial *talapatr*, the embroidered fan that monks hold before their faces when they are chanting. It showed up in a rather fetching picture published of me with a silly wide grin on my face. Obviously, being ordained was, for me, a lot of fun, like having Christmas in June.

Most men try to join the monkhood for *Vassa* (*phansa*) often mis-named 'Buddhist Lent.' *Vassa* is the rainy season that usually starts with the full moon in July and ends with the full moon in October.

The conditions of modern life, unforeseen by the ancient monks who set the Buddhist calendar, may make a full *Vassa* (three-month) ordination difficult or impossible. The period will not mesh well with the academic year for a student, so, rather than lose out on an entire year of studies, he may choose to be ordained for a shorter period. Or, his employer may not be able to spare him for the three months of the rains retreat, so if he goes into the temple at another more convenient time, he'll find his job waiting without a loss of seniority or other perks. Most Buddhist men in Thailand are farmers, so they can be ordained at the traditional time. Monks, by the way, count their seniority by how many *Vassa* they have lived in the monkhood.

The ordination procedure set down in the Buddha's time resembles that of a collegiate Greek-letter fraternity in an American university, with a secret vote of the other members to pass on the ordinand's application, the black-ball system. While realistically, all his qualifications have been studied and passed on beforehand, there is still in the ordination procedure a somewhat atrophied interrogation in memorized Pali to make sure there are no impediments to ordination. If you want to follow one of these services, acquire a copy of *Ordination Procedures*, which has Pali-English translations.

What Do I Do About Going to an Ordination?

The soon-to-be-ordained monk will find a moment to hand you a printed card announcing his ordination day and time, the temple at which the ceremony will be performed, and a printed schedule of the events: feeding of the chapter (group) of monks; a sermon in Thai to the assembled guests; and the ordination parade to the chapel. The names of the sponsors will also appear.

It is very much like an invitation to a wedding in the West, except that at some place on the card it will say, "*The ordinand requests your forgiveness of any offence by thought, word, or deed that he may have committed.*" With a polite *wai* he will extend this card to you, holding it between his hands. You accept it and can say, "Of course, you're forgiven," or "There was nothing to forgive." Or you can merely smile and say, "Thank you." A fairly strict Buddhist may say, "*Kho anumo-dana,*" which is a very formal way of saying thanks for the chance he has given you to help him, and thus make merit in your own life. It is the same situation discussed earlier: when you offer food to the monk in the morning, he will never thank you, for he has given you a chance to practice *dâna* ('generosity'), one of the Buddhist's virtuous acts, and thus to make merit.

On the other hand, when a monk leaves the robes to return to his layman's life, this is a cause for regret, and it is definitely not polite to ask the reason for his leaving the monkhood. After all, Thais believe that being a monk is better than anything else. So if he has to give up

that life, it is unfortunate. Or it may be a touchy subject. If the monk has misbehaved and been invited to leave the Order, it is best not to refer to it at all. Even if he has done nothing wrong but circumstances force him to return to lay life, that alone is unfortunate. No inquiry is best here.

You may, of course, find out the Thai way, which is quietly to ask a third party who may know the story. But that may skid very close to spreading gossip, so be careful even in that.

When you are handed the invitation to the ordination, there are two acceptable responses. One is to donate money to the would-be monk. This means you will probably not be attending the ceremony, but you're willing to help with expenses. The custom is to put money in a white envelope with your name on it. Give it to the ordinand and wish him well.

How Much Money?

That depends upon the relationship between the two of you. You can give as much as you want, but let the sum of money be in multiples of three: thus, thirty baht is all right for poor people to give. For most donations, 300 baht is adequate; it's not too little. You can, if you wish, donate 600 or 900 baht. The rule might be, the less intimate your relationship, the smaller the donation.

Do you attend the ceremony or not? If it is being held far away and is not convenient for you, it will depend on your free time and the availability of transport. But, if you have the time and inclination, then go and have a good time. Don't be put off by the intense informality where you might have expected sober-sidedness. Thais like to play. They seize on most opportunities to do so, and an ordination is no exception. For one, it's a happy occasion. Only in the chapel, during the service, is everyone very serious. Be careful about going into the chapel to sit, particularly down in front. You'll get a good view and hear everything, but what if your legs cramp? (You'll be sitting on your heels.) Can you beat a polite but quick retreat to the door?

Remember the rules you may have learned already. Don't extend your feet out towards the monks or the images. Keep your knees bent and your legs pulled back. As for prostrations and responses, you may simply sit there quietly. One recommendation from an old-timer at monastic functions: if you intend to stay in the chapel for the ceremony, find a pillar to lean back on. You'll have a much more comfortable time of it, and you'll see some Thais doing the same.

It is more than likely that a luncheon will be served at the temple. The monks normally eat first because they have a noon-time limit to be finished for the day. Then all the guests get to eat. Even if you don't eat any food, thank people for inviting you and be sure, before you leave, to say a respectful goodbye to the new monk.

What Should I Wear to an Ordination?

There is no need for suits and neckties or special dress for the ladies. Polite dress would include slacks and shirt or slacks and blouse. No hats, no gloves, and if you come down to it, even shoes are not necessary because you remove them outside the chapel. Sandals to be left in the doorway or on the porch outside are fine. Ladies should not wear tight skirts. As for colours, as this is not a funeral, coloured and flowered blouses are fine. For the men, slacks of any colour.

Photography is generally unobjectionable, but be sure to have sufficient film and batteries. Including the entry parade and dancing, three circumambulations of the chapel, the entry of the ordinand and the tossing-away of coins, then the service itself and the parade out—the total time should be about an hour.

There could be comedic elements such as the village women and their enthusiastic prancing about, the 'big heads' bowing and swaying about, or the parading of the new monk's robes and gifts. You might get some unforgettable snapshots or videos.

Death and the Funeral That Follows

If ordination represents the initiation of a Buddhist man as he enters upon his religious life as a *bhikkhu*, so his death leads to the funeral that is meant to send him off to yet another life, should there be another into which he can be reborn.

Women, of course, without having been *bhikkhu* or even extra-devout laywomen, join in dying the same way, with the same prospects.

At your workplace, or from your domestic employees and, of course, from your Thai friends and acquaintances, you may receive a card similar to the ordination invitation. This new card, printed in black, will be an invitation to the funeral sessions and, at their end, to the cremation—if there is to be one any time soon.

The time between the monks' chanting sessions for the funeral and the cremation may be a matter of days, months, or even a year or two, depending upon a number of elements: the social rank of the deceased (the higher the rank, the longer the mourning period), the whereabouts of parents or offspring, or the wish to perform several cremations together. This delay between death and cremation often catches expats by surprise, and you may have many questions about the customs involved.

When you are invited, you may, as with an ordination, return an envelope with a monetary gift; again, multiples of 300 baht are appropriate in most cases. You may do this at the time you receive the invitation, or wait until you attend the ceremony. Just watch and see who has been designated as the collector of these envelopes and follow along.

The invitation will tell you who has died as well as who is sponsoring the various elements of the funeral (usually relatives, the employer, or professional associations). It will also tell you where and when the ceremonies will take place, usually in a Buddhist *wat*. Even expat Christians are cremated in Buddhist *wats* because of the facilities available. Muslims, who do not cremate, have their own cemeteries. Chinese funerals usually take place in Buddhist temples, and the dead are interred in cemeteries where the *feng shui* ('geomancy') is auspicious.

Whether the funeral is a royally sponsored affair will also be indicated on the card. This may indicate what degree of formality in dress is required. As a whole, funerals are a lot dressier than ordinations.

In an earlier time, it was a tradition that a dying person would listen to chanting by a chapter (the proper word for group or gathering) of monks so that the last thing heard in this life would be the words of the Buddha's teaching. This was to assure that the dying person was in a proper and wholesome frame of mind to approach the end of life.

If the body can be made presentable, it will be laid out on a bed or cot, neatly dressed in the best clothing or uniform. One hand is left to lie over the edge so that the mourners may line up, approach the body, and (bowing or kneeling) pour a conch-shell of lustral (holy) water over the palm. This is a way of asking for forgiveness of the dead for 'any offence in thought, word, or deed.' It is, you'll notice, the same formula used in the ordination situation. It also is a formal farewell to the dead.

Should there be royal involvement in the funeral, the hand washing will end when water arrives from the palace to be used by the officials who represent the king. Lustral water plays a similar role in Buddhism to the holy water of the Roman Catholics, and has been blessed in a ceremonial manner by monks or by the king.

Small children and pregnant women do not as a rule attend funerals. It is believed by some that the ghosts or spirits that may be present constitute a danger to the unborn or infant. Many Thais believe that a dispossessed spirit may be seeking a new home to occupy. In fact, the bodies of people who have been killed before their time (as in a road accident) are, in some parts of Thailand, buried straightaway, and exhumed two years later for the traditional ceremonies. They are considered too dangerous as their ghosts, *phi* (pronounced 'pee'), are dissatisfied and hungry for vengeance on the luckless living. After two years and some ritual appeasement, the *phi* will go away and the living can get on with the proper funeral and cremation.

After the hand anointing, the body will be removed to a proper wooden coffin, often of plain planks. The lid will be nailed down and then the whole thing will be lifted up onto an altar-like catafalque. The plain coffin will be covered with ornate panelling and everything buried in flowers. To one side, supported on an easel, there is usually an enlarged photograph of the deceased. Before it will be a kneeling place (the prie-dieu of Western tradition) and a candle and incense stick receptacle. This arrangement will remain until all the chanting sessions have finished—three, seven, fifty, a hundred nights, or more. The funeral card will tell you how many sessions there will be. Chanting usually begins at 7:30 or 8:00 p.m. and may take an hour.

If the funeral is for an important or high-ranking person, the body is not placed lying down in its coffin, but is seated in a foetal position in a full-body-sized funeral urn. With knees drawn up to the chin, the body is impaled on a drain, and quicksilver may be poured into the mouth to encourage faster drying of the corpse. The body fluids, called *sanies*, drip into a container of sandalwood sawdust that, at the time of cremation, will be scattered around or under the corpse.

When her HRH the Princess Mother of Thailand died in July 1995, tens of thousands of people signed the condolence book and paid respects to her at an altar-like edifice in the palace that was crowned with the great urn. Born a commoner in 1900, she was the mother of two monarchs (Rama VIII and the present king, Rama IX) and so was granted full royal rank and the ceremonies commensurate with it. The formal court mourning period for her was 100 days, but her cremation was scheduled for March 1996, at Sanam Luang, the great open space before the Grand Palace. An ornate structure was built to house her funeral urn for the ceremonies, and the elaborate, gilded funeral carriage was pulled in procession to carry the urn to the crematorium.

Funerals are generally in three parts: the hand anointing and boxing of the body, the formal evening chanting sessions, and the cremation. The farewell to the deceased in the coffin is generally done by approaching the catafalque, kneeling, lighting one joss-stick, *wai*ing with it, and placing it in its sand bowl. You then withdraw on your knees backwards, stand, and depart to leave room for the next mourner. Watch others as long as you need to until you're sure of yourself.

The chapter of four monks will then file in, take their seats on a platform, lift their *talapatr*, and begin to recite the service in a manner less melodious than rhythmic. The leading monk will indicate in a few syllables which chant will be delivered; the others catch on and join in.

While the chanting is done in several sections with a pause between each, the audience members sit quietly holding their hands in a polite *wai*. Some people may chat quietly or busy themselves with laying out gifts for the monks and preparing the traditional drinks and snacks for the mourners. It has become a practice in Bangkok, where traffic makes it very difficult to get around, to shorten the chanting period. At one time it was at least twenty minutes per section. But Bangkokians now listen to three sections that are about ten minutes each. Upcountry and suburban funerals will usually keep to the chanting of the more traditional and longer stanzas.

After the chanting has ended, the host and others of the family or mourners will approach the monks' platform to offer gifts. Women lay theirs on a cloth that the monk places before him so that he doesn't touch the offering at the same moment as female hands. He indicates he is accepting it for himself by touching the offering cloth. Men can offer their gifts directly into the hands of the monk. The gifts may be elaborate decorated trays, or simple robes, but usually something the monk can find useful in monastic life: a bathing robe, towel, soap, washing powder, toothbrush and toothpaste, a small teapot, cup and saucer, boxed tea leaves, matches, candles, and so on.

There is then a chant of blessing, and the monks withdraw to their quarters while the crowd disperses. Many mourners may attend two or more evenings of the scheduled chanting, and almost everyone will attend the cremation whenever it takes place.

My own rule is to attend the hand anointing if the deceased was close to me, then at least one of the chanting sessions, especially if I am included as a host for the evening—such as representing my department at the university where I taught. I then attend the cremation, particularly because I like the Mon funeral music played by the *phinphaat* orchestra, often accompanied by a singer-chanter.

The Mon music is more resonant than Thai music and is generally quite loud. (Mons, by the way, are an ethnic group to the west and north of Bangkok, but today live mostly in Eastern Burma. Their kingdom never really took hold, and has now disappeared from the map. But they consider their history sacred and have been one of the major ethnic groups fighting the military junta ruling in Burma).

Just beside the entrance to the *sala* ('pavillion' or 'hall') where the coffin rests in splendour on its catafalque, there will be a large signboard on which are listed the dates for chanting and the names of the sponsors, as well as the time and date of the cremation. These boards are inevitably in Thai so don't be shy about asking for translations. As far as that goes, if you happen upon the *sala* and don't know whose funeral it is, ask a bystander. Or the host may come out to talk to you and invite you to sit down and enjoy a soft drink or snack with everyone else, even if you aren't known to them. Thais are very generous and open in this way.

After the chanting has been completed, and if the cremation will take place long after, the coffin will be removed for storage until it is brought out again for the cremation rites.

Five p.m. is a popular time for cremations, although they may take place at other hours. The cremation is the most important and colourful of the funeral ceremonies. At this affair, for which a notice may also have appeared in the newspapers, a monk will deliver a sermon. There may also be performances by a band and dancers, a play or movie, or, in country districts rather than in the city, a display of fireworks. In other words, there is nothing gloomy or lugubrious about Thai funerals.

An American teacher friend of mine married a Thai woman who opened a seamstress shop, employing several girls. One of these had a soldier boyfriend. Something happened between them and she wanted to break up. The disappointed suitor delivered a beautifully wrapped gift to the shop, supposedly to beg her to come back to him. The gift was carried into the shop, and the girl it was intended for dove headfirst out the window.

The gift turned out to be a bomb, which went off, killing three of the other girls.

My friend was obligated by custom to sponsor the funerals and cremations of his wife's dead employees. He was doing his duty, Thai-style, but he felt distressed over the whole situation and showed it. He wept during the service until his wife dug him in the ribs and hissed, "Don't act so sad. It's a funeral!"

At the proper time after the sermon and performances, some prominent mourner (it could be you!) will be invited to place aromatic sandalwood under the coffin. If the coffin has not yet been removed and slid into the oven, then it is a symbolic gesture. If it has been removed and placed in the burner, your bit of sandalwood may bear the first flame for the cremation. If you are summoned to approach the coffin or the oven, don't feel shy. No one will let you make a mistake. Someone, perhaps the son of the deceased, will guide you through every step.

At the door to the burning oven, hold the sandalwood in your hands before you, *wai,* and then place it under the coffin or into the flames if the fire has already been lit. *Wai* again, step back, and walk down the stairs. At this point, before you leave, someone will hand you the funeral

gift. This may be a book about, or by, the deceased, or perhaps about some specialized aspect of Thai culture. These are quite collectible and, after a short time, may even appear in second-hand bookstalls.

In some formal funerals, when the orchestra reaches the peak of its music and the crowd shuffles towards the oven to place their sandalwood bits, a keener may sometimes join in to wail during the placing of the corpse and coffin in the fire. His is a sound that can send shivers up your backbone. This custom, still common in India, has almost disappeared in modern Thailand.

In more rural locations, rockets that spurt flame and smoke may be used, as they follow a cord or wire strung around the outdoor cremation place to the coffin to ignite the flames.

It is customary for a coffin to be opened shortly before it is placed in the flames or oven. To omit this is to cause comment amongst the public. It is all right to photograph at funerals, even to take a flash picture of the corpse in the coffin. What a viewer will behold is a slightly shrunken figure, often with a dark green hue that is the result of the embalming fluid. I have noticed that most expats avoid this viewing. I do, too. I prefer to remember the deceased in better days. But most Thais are rather curious and will peer into the coffin and perhaps place small envelopes or cards inside. These are personal and private remembrances and are not required.

What Should I Wear to a Funeral?

For Thais: all black, all white, or a mix of the two, unless they are eligible to wear the all-white uniform of a civil servant. Military people wear the appropriate uniforms. Women wear a black dress and shoes. For expats, a dark suit for men or dark slacks and a white shirt. If you were close to the deceased it would be good to wear a black tie, as well. Any dark and sober colour is acceptable, but no one should wear red. Amongst Chinese (and therefore many Thais), red is a symbol of good fortune and thus not acceptable for funerals, despite the often cheerful atmosphere.

If you're going to be staying in Thailand long, have your black funeral dress or outfit ready for use at any time. Many Thais only meet at funerals, which are therefore socially important affairs. There is a Thai saying, 'We only meet at funerals now,' which implies we're getting older and seeing our old friends and colleagues off.

The day after the cremation, the family will send representatives to the temple to collect the relics that survived the flames. These may be tossed into the sea or saved at home in a miniature brass *stupa* or *chedi*. They may also be put in a larger *stupa* or *chedi* in a temple or even in an alcove in the temple wall that will be marked by a stone plaque with the photograph and details of the deceased.

There is little tendency to repeat anniversaries of deaths except for royalty. The dead are gone to their just rewards, perhaps a new life, the conditions of which will be determined by the life they have just departed. Memories of the deceased are private affairs.

Weddings

It is quite likely that during your stay in Thailand you will receive an invitation to a wedding. Since Thai weddings are fairly straightforward affairs, they should present little problem. The wedding announcement will tell who is sponsoring whom, when, where, with reception or dinner to follow at such-and-such restaurant or hotel. Because of the problems of catering, most wedding parties are not conducted in people's homes.

There is no such thing as a specifically Buddhist wedding. This is due to the fact that this 'religion' does not officially recognize marriage as sacred, although monks may attend to chant and bless the couple and to enjoy the luncheon before returning to their temple laden with the usual gifts.

The essence of the wedding is a presentation of money—the bride price. The groom-to-be must pay the bride's father, ostensibly for having raised her well, protected her, and for the loss of her services to him in his old age. The figure may run from a few thousand baht into really big money, with gifts of gold and jewels, as well. Usually this payment is part of the engagement ceremony.

If the father of the bride likes the young man, he will keep the price reasonable. If he has not a fondness for the soon-to-be son-in-law, he may set an extortionate figure he knows the groom cannot meet. The danger here is that a determined couple may then elope and Dad gets nothing. After a time, the groom may bring his pregnant bride back and threaten to return her to her father. This may well cause paternal panic! He does not want to try to marry off a 'used' daughter, one who has been carried off and then rejected. Of course, it's a manoeuvre by the couple to get Dad to accept the groom rather than face a scandal. Once a child is born, however, the grandfather may melt in the baby's delightful gurgles and chuckles, and the money part may be forgotten.

It may seem odd, but the groom, the bride, and her father all want the bride price to be as high as possible. The groom will strut around bragging that he paid so-many-thousands for his wife; the girl will brag to her friends how much her man paid for her; and Dad will feel happy with a large payment. But it doesn't really work that way with some couples. In some cases, the amount will be set, but it will be lent by the

bride's father to the young man, who will merely return it. Everyone saves face this way.

The wedding ceremony is straightforward. As you walk in the door, it is customary to present the bride and groom with an envelope containing a donation, or present them with a wedding gift. The monks will chant their blessing and the couple will kneel on a prie-dieu. An elder relative will then place over their heads a long garland made with flowers or sacred string. This garland will tie the groom and the bride together. They will kneel on the pri-dieu and the senior guests (all those older than them) will pour lustral water over their *wai*ed hands, murmuring a blessing as they do so.

At my eldest son's wedding, the floral yoke-like garland that tied him to his wife slipped over his head and around his neck, exactly like a hanging noose. While at the time we all enjoyed his discomfiture, it may have been a bad omen. His wife turned out to be very bossy, and, in the end, they divorced.

At the party following the ceremony, the more important guests will be invited to make a blessing speech and (as so often in Thai social affairs), to sing unaccompanied by any instrumental assistance. If you are going to attend many Thai parties, prepare a song or two so you don't have to squirm in your chair, embarrassed and trying to beg off. Most Thais know some songs so they can hardly believe that you may not.

In one of my first teaching assignments I was having a terrible time encouraging the students to speak English. I asked questions about the lesson ('The British Post Office') and everyone avoided eye contact while I pleaded for some response. Finally, a girl at the top of the amphitheatre-like risers raised her hand.

"Yes, miss?" I called out.

"Will you sing us a song?"

I am no threat to Caruso's reputation, but I happen to know one verse of a rather tuneless Tennessee hillbilly ballad. So I howled (nasally, in proper hillbilly style) that,

"My maaaan walked dooooown the railroad traaaack,

A quarteh of a maaaaaille from taooooooown.

The traaaaain hit him squaaaaere in the baaaack,

His baaaawdy ain't neveh bin faoooooooound."

It was a hit. I had done my social duty. And I must confess, I have never been asked for an encore. Never.

The rest of the wedding party will probably be dedicated to eating. Thais often like to entertain with a Chinese-style banquet of many courses, so be sure not to stuff yourself early.

At some point, before you leave, your hosts will give you a small souvenir of the occasion, a bottle opener or cigarette lighter or key chain, with the names of the bride and groom on them and the date. As everywhere, you wish your hosts all the best in life when you leave.

Other Groups, Customs, and Traditions

Chinese

You may find variations in certain celebrations. Chinese weddings tend to be grand affairs, noisy and colourful, and with enough food to feed a whole village. Chinese funerals may be of the kind called *kong tek*, which are also colourful. Once, I had an undertaker friend who would call me when there was a particularly big Chinese funeral at his temple, which housed a large, solid-gold Buddha image. Grabbing up a couple of friends who were interested in Chinese customs, we'd taxi off to Wat Plapplachai (not far from the railway station) and go in to watch the ceremony. As in Thai funerals, there are several pauses in the goings-on.

In one of these *kong tek* funerals, we arrived at an awkward moment and were waved to sit and rest in a nearby pavilion. We stepped into it and, luckily, no one sat down. One of our members reached to pull a chair out, and it lifted up easily in her hand. She was startled at the near weightlessness of it. As it turned out, all the furniture in the pavilion was made of paper: table, chairs, radio, teapot, you name it, everything was of paper to be burned later so these things would accompany the dead into the heavens. It's a good thing we didn't really plonk ourselves down without checking first.

You can distinguish Chinese affairs by the copious use of red: red lettering, red hangings, red and gold whatever, everywhere. And the noise: banging gongs, shrill flutes and whistles, cymbals. The first time I heard this kind of music, I thought a terrible car accident had happened in the street. It turned out to be the overture of a Chinese opera. The Thais (who aren't exactly silent themselves!) find the Chinese noisy, particularly when they talk to each other on a bus, or elsewhere.

Muslims

Thailand has about six million Muslims, mostly in the deep south near the Malaysian border, although there are many communities in and around Bangkok. In the wee hours of the mornings in some districts you can hear the muezzin's call to prayer from the minaret's loudspeakers.

One way to identify Muslims is by the presence of Arabic lettering on taxi windshields, windows of food shops, over the gates into Muslim religious schools, and by their dress. This last is especially true on Fridays,

when the men will wear caps or turbans and colourful sarongs. Thai Muslim women and girls may wear the *hijab*, a scarf over the head that frames the face. Less often, you may see women completely covered with the black *burqa*. As in other countries with Muslim populations, it is best if men don't pay too much attention to Muslim women. It may be quickly resented.

Most Thais know very little about Muslims, and, years ago regarded them as foreigners. The term used for Muslims is *khaek*, the same as the Thai word for 'guest.' Thais refer to all South Asians: Indians—both Hindu and Muslim—Pakistanis, Bangladeshis, and Sri Lankans, and Middle Easterners as *khaek*, in the same way they generically refer to all white Westerners as *farang*.

During the Arabic month of Ramadan, scrupulous Muslims abstain from eating, drinking, and sexual relations during the daytime. Then at sundown, they may start parties that last till dawn when the prohibitions come into effect again. As the Arabic calendar is lunar, it is shorter than the solar year by about 11 days. Ramadan and other Muslim observations move ahead accordingly each solar year, working their way through the calendar. Ramadan is announced on the radio and television and in newspapers that have Muslim readers. This religious observation ends with the feast Ei-ul-Fitr.

Generally, Thai Buddhists and Muslims live together peacefully. But at times there are sharp edges to their relationships. Unlike the Chinese, who eat pork and drink liquor, follow Buddhist traditions, and intermarry and mix easily with Buddhist Thais, the Muslims find that their social and religious restrictions sometimes limit their contact with other Thais.

Following Thai ideas about keeping one's cool and not getting worked up over things, most Thai Muslims have avoided the harsh excesses of some Islamic groups against others. But that does not ensure that overseas meddling into Muslim communities in the south of Thailand might not one day result in the same tensions that afflict the Southern Philippines.

Most Thai Muslims attend special schools where religion is taught. They also learn the Yawi language (Malay as written in Arabic letters). In the not-so-distant past, government officers assigned to Muslim areas created problems by their ignorance of Islam.

A country with Hindus, Christians, Sikhs, and Chinese, all with their imported customs and with a vast array of animistic beliefs, should display tolerance and willingness to yield in some matters. Thailand has shown a great forbearance for religious variety, and Thais can be proud that they have no black record for intolerance of other's ideas.

One exception to this rule does exist, however. That is a love affair between a Muslim girl and a non-Muslim man. As Muslim girls are forbidden to marry outside of their religion, whereas men are free to do so, sometimes a critical point is reached. Disappointed, jealous, or rejected lovers wreaking revenge, or home-wrecking adventurers getting between spouses—these tend to produce newspaper headlines and grief all around. Over-protective parents and their headstrong offspring share in the blame as well, but the troubles between people are usually more personal than attributable to religion.

Christians

Christians have been in Thailand for centuries. The first to come were Portuguese Catholics, as Portugal conquered bits and pieces of India, Sri Lanka, and Southeast Asia, and began to control trade. Thai kings had cordial relationships with Portuguese priests and officials, and allowed them to establish settlements in Ayuddhaya and elsewhere. Today we are so used to English being the second language of this part of the world that we forget almost all business and politics was once conducted in Portuguese, up into the nineteenth century, until Portugal's real influence faded away. The Portuguese kings sent expeditions and missionaries to this part of the world, and built churches and forts and traders' 'factories.' They also established Catholic communities, some of which still exist.

In the early 1800s, Protestant missionaries began to appear in Thailand. They were fortunate in that Prince Mongkut was one of the possible heirs to the throne. He was approachable and interested in the world, not isolated inside his palace walls as the reigning king was. Prince Mongkut received missionaries, sea captains, and other outsiders, and managed to learn English and Latin, as well as much about science. He was a voracious reader and enjoyed a wide correspondence with important figures in Europe and America.

Missionaries, because they stayed and became part of the foreign community—bringing talents that the prince believed were needed here—played a large part in hospital building and operation, education,

and book printing. When Prince Mongkut acceded the throne (it was a disputed succession; one of the elements held in his favour was his intimate knowledge of foreigners and their ways), he followed his interests even more. He died in 1868, but the transformation of Siam was well underway as a result of his 37-year reign. Christians continued to play a small but significant role in that transformation.

Since then, Christian missionaries have been welcomed to Thailand, although they have never had much success in making converts to their religion. They have set up churches, schools, and communities amongst the Chinese and various tribal peoples, but Buddhist Thais have never shown much more than polite, yet distant, interest in the religion.

The Roman Catholics currently have two Thai archbishops, one of whom is also a cardinal; eight other bishops; and more than 500 Thai priests. They are very well established in their churches and seminaries. At one point, the Church hierarchy petitioned the Thai government to allow more

European priests to enter the country and work, but they were refused on the grounds that the Catholics have had 350 years to establish themselves and should be producing Thai priests in sufficient numbers by now.

Certain features of Christian society strike Thais particularly. One of these is Christmas. It is much less a Christian celebration amongst the Thai public than a chance to go shopping, to meet Santa Claus, and to have parties. The finer details (reindeer, chimneys, carolling, and the crèche, let alone baby Jesus) are usually ignored, but gift buying and giving most definitely is not. The reason is that, while Christmas is only partially understood, it falls between the celebration of the present king's birthday on December 5th and the international New Year. Illuminations for the king's birthday are still hanging at Christmas and remain through the New Year celebrations, giving Bangkok a festive appearance. Most Thais I know think that Christmas is *farang* New Year!

Animism

Thais believe that there are many other kinds of (usually) unseen creatures that share our world (and maybe other worlds, as well). They are thought to live in rocks, trees, ponds, lakes, and just about every other natural feature. The impulse to believe in this is ancient, going back to the beginnings of the human family, and is expressed in all cultures.

Thais believe that trees are inhabited by spirits, or the tree has a soul. People sometimes believe that talking to their houseplants makes the plants healthier. This type of animism is so intertwined with Buddhist beliefs that many foreigners can be forgiven for imagining the two are the same. They are not.

Twenty or so years ago, the electrical authority in Thonburi wanted to run power lines down Phrannok Road towards the ferry docks at the end. To make a straight line, a great and very old tree would have to be chopped down. This prospect stirred up the neighbourhood. Everyone knew that that tree housed a benevolent spirit that had often given out winning numbers for the lottery. The local people had decorated the tree with saffron-coloured cloth bands, and often made candle and incense offerings at the tree's small altar stand. The idea that anyone could cut down that tree for the mere reason of stringing wires was totally unacceptable. A protest was organized.

The resolution was, I thought, very Thai. The electric people sent a representative to explain that the wires might be strung to pass *around* the tree, but to do so would require the erection of two more poles, and that would cost the electric authority about 40,000 baht more than the allocated budget. The neighbours got together and raised the sum, which was paid to the authority. The two extra poles were erected, the wires strung along the street at an angle, and the tree was saved.

I haven't been to Phrannok for years now, but I'd bet that old tree is still giving out winning lottery numbers and exam answers, as it has for generations.

Almost anywhere you go, you are liable to run across these orange-clothed trees, so animism is still hale and hearty in Thailand—although it doesn't always have such a successful ending as in the case above. During the all-too-regular national uproars over logging in the last remaining forests of the kingdom, local monks and the village people will get together to ordain trees into the monkhood, wrapping them with the proper cloth to show they are to be protected from the chainsaw gangs. Animism, unfortunately, does not always win out over capitalism when it comes to quick profits for the logging companies.

In some parts of Thailand, men or women are believed to become inhabited by a spirit, or *deva* or *thep*, an angelic being. Or perhaps we could say the *deva* has taken on the human form. Whichever is the case, there was one well-known episode in Samrong, Eastern Bangkok, on the old road leading to the Gulf resorts. This possessed victim was inhabited by a *rukkhathep*, a 'tree fairy' or male nymph, who, however, had none of the delicate, lovely qualities associated with fairies and nymphs.

He was an overweight, short man of almost forty years, who commuted daily from his house in Bangkapi to the corrugated-iron-roofed 'heaven' in Samrong where he held sessions with believers. These were people from the nearby port, factory workers, fishermen, pirates, prostitutes, and a sprinkling of university students, gangsters, and monks. From his twisted mouth and facial expression, I assumed he had had a stroke that had partially paralyzed his left side. A steady red drool of betel juice stained his lips and chin. It also dropped onto his white T-shirt, giving it a rather bloody look.

At the time, there was a BBC TV unit in Thailand led by Brian Barron. I got involved when the British Embassy called me to set up a meeting between Brian and the tree fairy. Brian had originally come to Thailand to film some of the action on the Thai-Cambodia border, but all was quiet at that time. Somehow he heard about this phenomenon in Samrong. My assistant, Khun Viroj, and I drove out to the tin-roofed 'heaven,' which was hotter than hell. We made our arrangements and reappeared at the instructed time with Brian, the cameraman, and a couple of technicians.

We took off our shoes and bowed our way through the seated crowd to the edge of the altar, a series of shelves laden with images of gods, kings, and one very obvious Kewpie doll with yellow hair. Incense pots and candle holders were scattered about. Prominent on a lower shelf in front of the fairy was an ink stamping set and what appeared to be a set of cookie cutters, larger than my grandmother used to use. The 'possessed' man used these stamp patterns on his applicants, who would withdraw to one side of 'heaven' to have themselves tattooed in that pattern.

The crowd was thick and not exactly welcoming, but we pushed our way forward on our knees, Viroj and I leading the British party. Arriving before the fairy, Viroj and I did our best deep prostration (the floor was a mess) and saluted the *rukkhathep*. Viroj introduced us one at a time and the fairy returned our *wai* in response. The smell of the old incense and the stale air breathed by so many people, plus the unappealing, messy appearance of the fairy were enough to nauseate the script girl.

We held a public interview, interrupted by his suppliants who were requesting help in finding lost items, lost lovers, securing new ones, and a myriad of other matters. He took care of them all by distributing amulets, bits of rock, a pre-printed light singlet, and plain bits of cloth with woodblock printing on them and the curlicue letters of Khmer that many Thais seek out as sacred inscriptions.

The tree fairy offered to send a message of peace and well-being to the good English folk, but he refused to allow himself to be photographed. We could talk and film anything else, even his altar, but not him, which was tricky because to film the altar, a full blast of lamplight from the crew would have to be used, and some of it spilled onto the fairy, as well.

People muttered conspiratorially in low tones as the camera was directed around the hut, preceded by the light boom, and some probably did not understand that the cameraman was indeed not filming the *deva*, who was caught in the light.

The rest of the story sounds more like *The National Enquirer* or the tabloid *Sun* in the UK, but it is true. On our second visit to his hut, the fairy was 'cooking' his believers, those who were delivered to his den on pallets and stretchers, unable to walk and looking more dead than alive. Each one in turn was laid before the *deva*, who rested his own foot on a metal plate set over a glowing charcoal-burning brazier, the kind used to broil steaks and sausages.

A smell similar to charred bacon was overwhelming. Wisps of smoke arose from his foot as he lifted it and placed it on the forehead of the sick person. An assistant spread a towel over the patient's forehead so there was no direct contact between the seared sole of the *rukkhathep* and the patient's skin.

I saw no reaction from any of the patients.

Brian's team filmed and the murmuring grew louder, especially from the tough-looking chunky women whom I took for prostitutes from Paknam, the nearby port. All of a sudden, one of them stood and pushed me against a pillar, hissing through a burst of confusion, "Take care! It's going to *din*!"

I had no time to ask what 'din' meant. I'd only just heard the word from my son who 'dinned' at a discotheque near his university. I thought it meant to dance, perhaps. Before I had time to think through what she had said, something heavy slammed against me, smashing me into the post, and then was gone instantly. My glasses had disappeared, the breath was knocked out of me, my feet tangled on a camera box.

All I saw was a body—human, I presumed—that *flew* at about chest level around the room knocking people down like tenpins, clearing a large area in front of the altar. I had no idea what had 'dinned' or what that was meant to describe. I slid my back down the pillar into a squat and fished around for my glasses, trying to get a foot loose from the metal camera boxes I was stuck in. When I got up, people were milling about. Brian signalled for us to leave and, paying our briefest respects to the *rukkhathep*, we made for the door.

I hadn't seen the BBC film, though a friend in England wrote that she had been startled to see me on a Saturday television show. Later I found that 'din' (whatever it may mean in a disco) is a rapid movement or thrashing about. In this case, it was said to have been a tiger doing it.

As this information leads to several interesting questions, I'll simply leave it till you begin exploring for yourself. You may also have the experience of being knocked flat by a tiger! Who knows?

Spirit Houses

Almost everywhere you go in Thailand you will notice small shrines, like miniature Buddhist chapels, standing on pillars. They resemble an ornate birdhouse but often are far fancier creations of spires and peaked roofs, floridly and brilliantly decorated in red and gilt as well as other colours. These are called *san phra bhumi* (*san prah poom*, or 'spirit houses'), and this is exactly what they are, homes for land spirits.

Made of wood or cement, spirit houses should bear some relationship in fanciness with the house or building they 'represent,' so the spirit will feel comfortable. A small, simple wooden house will do for the spirit of the land where a farming family may have its own simple wooden house. A great fancy Khmer temple-like affair houses the spirit where a bank headquarters has been erected. While not universal, these spirit houses

are to be found just about anywhere *except* in a Buddhist *wat*. But even still, you may find older spirit houses near the wall of a *wat*, or many of them lying in a heap under a wide-spreading tree. These have been discarded in favour of newer, more luxurious spirit houses.

The *san phra bhumi* is treated like a shrine, and offerings of food, fruit, flowers, candles, incense, and sometimes whiskey or a whole pig's head may be laid on the porch of the shrine or on a table set before it. It may also be 'peopled' with tiny elephants, horses, and wee dancing girls. Most Thais (and many expats) honour these spirit houses even without knowing too much about the spirit in residence. It is part of the general essence of Brahmanism that underlies Thai spirituality.

125

Because they are not related to Buddhism, these shrines are not erected by Buddhist monks when they may come to bless your house or place of business. Rather, a Brahmin will set the requirements for placing your shrine and will carry out the ceremonies to invite the spirits to reside happily in it. The Thai Brahmin is not a member of some special caste as in India, but is trained in Brahmin beliefs and customs. He may also wear a white *chongkraben* and a white shirt or long upper garment embroidered with gold thread. Sometimes, he'll even wear white stockings and white shoes. Usually, he sports a little knot of hair on the back of his head. More important is his intimate knowledge of the Brahmin traditions, scriptures, and ceremonies.

Some big city hotels, banks, or mansions may host enormously fancy shrines, before which large offerings are made. The Bangkok Bank, for example, had two shrines at its former head office. This is because the bank building had housed the Japanese secret police during the Second World War and it was believed that victims of police interrogation and torture were buried on the property. The extra shrine was meant to protect the bankers and their customers from any especially unlucky spiritual influences. In these matters, more is considered better.

The offerings of food and drink, by the way, may be consumed by ordinary mortals after the spirits have had their fill of the essences. Ants may crawl up the supporting pillar, and birds may descend on the altars for an auspicious snack, as well. No one will gainsay them. Who knows, perhaps the spirits inhabit other creatures as well, Thais say.

In villages, bungalow colonies, city apartment blocks, and suburban housing estates, there may be a central spirit house that anyone can honour. I once lived with one next door to my neighbours' house, and we could tell when something was up by how many of the villagers stopped off to make offerings and *wai* the shrine. It was particularly busy at university and school exam time and on the evenings before the national lottery draw took place. Every once in a while, I'd find the shrine laden with floral offerings and I knew that some prayer request had been fulfilled.

At my new house in Khlong Chan, we had to replace the simple old rickety spirit house with a fancy new one commensurate with the reconstruction we had done. We all honoured it as the Brahmin instructed, and several members of the family won the lottery in subsequent drawings. I won 8,000 baht, my biggest prize ever, but it only happened during the first month or so after we'd installed the new spirit house and invited the spirit to move in. My second son, Ott, uses his influence over the spirit to try and control the weather. It's impressive how often it comes out his way. Remember the saying, 'Someone up there likes me?' Maybe we should say, 'Someone out there—in our spirit house—looks over us.' It seems that way. It was also odd that to buy and install our new spirit house with gifts for the Brahmin and offerings for the spirit cost exactly 8,000 baht.

Christians may be interested to learn that at the ruins of the Portuguese colony in Ayutthaya, which date from the early sixteenth century, there is a spirit house dedicated to saints Pedro and Paulo (Peter and Paul). A Catholic-run school in Bangkapi has one dedicated to the Virgin Mary, as well. Those, then, should be considered shrines for saints rather than true spirit houses.

Brahmanism

This is the name we apply to the animistic beliefs that Thais share in common with the peoples of the Indian subcontinent, in particular the Hindus. As Christianity is an outgrowth of Judaism, so Hinduism, Buddhism, and Jainism are reform movements of Brahmanism. In all three of the later religions an important emphasis is given to *ahimsa*, the practice

of harmlessness toward all beings no matter how small and seemingly insignificant. The Hindus, for example, dropped the famous Vedic 'horse sacrifice' from a very important royal ceremony in Brahmanical practice because the Jains and the Buddhists both objected to the blood sacrifice of the horses. However, followers of Brahmanism in Nepal still practise animal sacrifices similar to that one.

While Jains carry on this *ahimsa* by going to great lengths to avoid injury to lesser creatures, Buddhist monks still hold to certain minor features of it, such as employing a screened funnel to keep microbes out of the water they use, or wrap cloth around taps for the same reason. Gandhi was a great employer of *ahimsa* for political purposes—ultimately gaining India, Pakistan, and Bangladesh their independence from Britain.

Brahmanical practices are few in Thailand. One is the use of 'holy water,' discussed previously. Another is the *sai sin*, a Brahmanical cord (looking to the uninitiated like plain white string, which it is) that conveys blessings as an electrical wire conveys electric power. There is also the mumbo-jumbo of magical expressions to change nature or control it. The Buddha opposed fortune-telling and ceremonial rites like these. He did not believe in priests and their incantations, or gurus of the type that sit cross-legged in caverns or on rocks above the Ganges and pontificate.

But it is true that Brahmanical pre-Buddhist beliefs and practices abound in Thailand, particularly in connection with nature and land spirits. A notable example is the Royal Ploughing Ceremony conducted in May at Sanam Luang in Bangkok, where representatives of the government plough the soil in the presence of the king and other members of the royal family. For an agricultural country, this is a very important occasion, made more so by the distribution of rice seed blessed by the king. It is also a ritual at which the royal *phra kho*, the 'king's cattle,' are used to predict future weather and abundance of certain crops. The 'Lord of the Plough' (often an official of the agriculture ministry) with his corps of 'Celestial Maidens' (other government employees) will perform the round-the-field ploughing and sowing of the blessed rice. The sacred cattle then 'choose' from amongst the grains, grass, water, or whiskey made available to them, to 'make their prediction' about crops in the coming year.

This colourful ceremony was abolished after the fall of the absolute monarchy and restored a decade or two later, some say for the benefit of tourists. With the first performance of the revived affair, the *phra kho* chose the whiskey and dashed off the field leading everyone on a wild chase through the city streets. Thai whiskey has a strong affect on animals, too!

You will notice no mention of Buddhist monks at the Ploughing Ceremony. That's because this occasion has nothing to do with Buddhism, so they're not participants.

The Brahmins, called 'Court Brahmins' when connected with palace affairs, perform part of the coronation of Thai kings and are in evidence in other ceremonies involving royalty. There is a long history behind the concept of the king-as-god. It is so ancient that it is full of pre-Buddhist ideas and activities, and would be worthy of a study itself. But most Thais are not much concerned about it. They do, however, recognize non-Buddhist elements in their practice of Buddhism and correctly identify them as *sasana phrahm*, 'Brahman religion.' But Thais do not object to them or regard them as elements that should be removed from a 'purified' Buddhism.

Thais are very pragmatic about such things and want to try whatever will work in the spiritual side of life. They have always been admirably tolerant of most religious practices. The only exceptions to this rule are religious beliefs or acts with political overtones, or perceived impoliteness toward Buddhism, the monarchy, or the king.

Ghosts

One of my university students wrote, "I know there aren't ghosts, but I am afraid of them." You cannot watch Thai television for one whole evening without seeing a ghost story. Coffins open by themselves and half-deformed creatures push the lid aside and rise slowly, awkwardly chasing the leading lady off the screen. Green, puffy, half-rotted features with staring eyes, clad in decayed rags, these pathetic characters lurch across the screen to the terrified screams of viewers—and not just maids and other simple folk. A dramatic technique has dogs seeing the ghosts, but the leading actors do not, so the tension builds. Another variation has the ghost take on the form of a beautiful woman who's about to wrap her bony arms around the handsome leading man. He must have a bad head cold because the smell of a ghost is usually said to be very noticeable, and unpleasant at that.

Thailand is home to several kinds of ghosts, according to specialists. Many are the unhappy dead, rising for some purpose like revenge.

Others are merely monstrous in their behaviour as well as appearance. One of the most colourful, and one I'd not like to meet on a dark night, is the *phi krasue*, a woman who is all head with entrails hanging out where her body used to join her neck. She—for *phi krasue* always take the female form—hovers around cemeteries and seeks dead bodies and human excrement to eat, or the luckless living. She is probably the most feared of all Thai ghosts, but that is hardly saying much. They are all frightening to the average Thai.

Phi tai hong is a ghost who is dissatisfied (usually having died in a horrible way) and feels an urge to take it out on the living. It might have been a child who died shortly after birth, or a woman who died in childbirth, or someone who died in an accident, or by murder or suicide. To *tai hong* is not a good way to die.

Preta, or *phi pret*, is a ghost recognized by Buddhism. One common description says that a *preta* has enormous appetites but only a needle

hole for a mouth. These appetites can be for food, power, money, sex . . . but they cannot be satisfied. It is a miserable existence, and a *preta* tends to be ill-tempered.

Ghosts are taken so seriously and believed in so universally to this day that housing near cemeteries is always much cheaper than the going market rates. Westerners living alone, anywhere in Thailand, are always asked, "Aren't you afraid of the ghosts?"

One evening some months after my brother Vit died, the house was filled with an unpleasant odour. It smelled familiar but I couldn't place it. As the smell persisted and grew stronger, my second son, Ott, flew out of his room, ran into mine, and declared, "Vit's here!" I have adopted the practice of giving Thais the benefit of the doubt in these matters, so I half-believed him. But it bothered me that the smell was familiar. Just to make sure, I went downstairs and out the gate, and there was my neighbour tending a fire on the pavement. And what was she burning? An automobile tyre.

As soon as I saw what she was up to, I called Ott to come downstairs. Reluctantly he came to the gate. "There's what's burning. See? A car tyre. That's all."

Ott looked at the fire and shook his head, but not in amazement at having mistaken a melting tyre for his uncle's presence. No, he ran inside the house calling for his brother and sister-in-law, both firm believers in ghosts, and announced, "Vit's been here. You can smell him!"

Not a person in my family would credit the stinking tyre for the source of the ghost's odour, though they all came out and sniffed.

"Can't you see that that's the smell? The tyre there," I repeated.

They all agreed the burning was smelly, but what they had noticed was a ghost smell. There is no convincing a true believer.

Amulets

Many Buddhists wear amulets. These small medallions that hang on a cord or chain around the neck, often encased in a gold box, are essential for mental well-being. To lose one (or have it stolen) can be a disaster. Ranging in price from a few baht to millions, some are very old family heirlooms. Others are considered especially effective and may mean a lot to a wearer. At ceremonies, monks may give them out, handing them to laymen, or dropping them onto the palms of a laywoman.

Some expats wear amulets, as well, and there are a few rules to keep in mind. One, explained below in more detail, is that a man's amulet is not to be placed in a position where it will be passed over by a woman's sexual organs, or clothing that has been in contact with them, such as panties or knickers. To do this can produce exceptionally negative reactions on the part of the amulet's owner.

The Amulet and the Underwear

Amulets are special; so much so that certain situations are nearly inconceivable. The story I now tell happened to a young Dutch couple who came to Bangkok some years ago to teach. They found a small two-storey wooden house in a narrow lane and rented it. This was cheap anywhere outside of a true slum, even then. There was no phone, no refrigerator, and practically no furniture. In the rainy season, which is about a quarter of the year, it was impossible for them to get their washing to dry. T-shirts, denim skirts, underwear, even handkerchiefs and, particularly, towels just stayed damp and eventually began to put out a mouldy smell.

The young Dutchman considered their predicament and came up with a solution. At a neighbourhood hardware store he bought a pair of pulley wheels and attachments, some screws, and enough rope to rig up a clothes-line. He also picked up a couple of dozen clothes-pegs. The couple discussed where to hang up this contraption, either in or around the house, but it was too small. The yard wasn't even big enough for a Chihuahua to scratch a flea in, so that wouldn't do either.

"Aha!" said the husband. "There's just the place! That pole on the other side of the lane. We'll fix one wheel on that and another on the balcony upstairs and run the rope between them."

Humming an old Dutch tune to herself, the wife carefully hung out the clothes on the new line and ran the clothes—creaking and screeching—to the pole on the other side of the lane.

Early the next morning they awoke to hear what they would later describe as a noise akin to the storming of Versailles. Loud talk, some shouting, and the sharp crack of something hard against their house got them up. They went to the window overlooking the lane. To their great surprise, they saw a crowd had gathered and was milling about, voicing a collective annoyance of some sort.

A man in the crowd saw the wife at the window, pointed and shouted. She didn't understand a word but felt frightened all the same. She turned to her husband, but several angry people had caught his attention. They talked at him urgently and persuasively.

Someone in the crowd shouted something in English. It sounded like "No panties!" Whatever that meant.

"No panties, no panties!" the crowd began to shout in measured unison. One man, wielding a long stick, tried to knock the panties loose from the line.

The Dutchman dashed down and appeared at the gate. Some of the neighbours were earnestly explaining something to him, while he looked sheepish and seemed to be apologizing profusely.

As he was busy at that, a boy shimmied up the pole, as the Dutchman had done the day before, and unhooked the new pulley. Being careful not to drop the wet clothes, he passed it over to a man who wadded everything up before tossing it to another man standing near the husband. The neighbours began to move towards the end of the lane, and soon it was cleared. The Dutchman leaned on his gate, waving farewell to the last of the concerned onlookers, several of whom waved back at him happily.

The tension had eased even faster than it had built up. Whatever was wrong with the clothesline, its removal ended the crisis. That evening, after they'd strung the clothesline inside the house, a neighbour came over to visit. He spoke English carefully and explained that no Thai man could ever walk under a clothesline holding women's underwear. Not even an empty one that he knew had once held a woman's nether garment.

The visitor quietly explained to the young Dutch couple that Thai men wore amulets on chains around their necks. These amulets conferred special protection to the wearers, and were treated with great respect.

One way to destroy the magical qualities of an amulet would be to place it beneath a woman's sexual organs or anything that had been in contact with them, such as panties. Even a bra was a no-no. In fact, in Thailand, a woman's nether garments or the real thing would 'blow' the powers of a man, with or without his amulets. So no woman would ever step over a man lying down, no matter the circumstances.

Thus the young Dutch couple resumed wearing not-quite-dry clothes and drying themselves with still-damp towels. But they had learned an important lesson!

A man may wear many amulets on a chain, perhaps a dozen, and it is commonly believed that he may need the protection they can confer on him. He may be a *nakieng* ('gangster') with a disposition to violence. Wearing many amulets may also mean that the bearer feels himself to be unlucky. Or he may just like the feeling of security in having them around his neck.

You will also see amulets dangling from the rear-view mirrors of cars, taxis, and most other motor vehicles in Thailand, to provide protection against accidents. Some drivers also stick them to the dashboard, along with miniature Buddha statues and pictures of particularly revered monks. Some of the displays can be quite elaborate.

Many people collect amulets, and there are specialist markets near several of the major *wats* in Bangkok. Go there, watch the shoppers or even make a purchase yourself. Just so long as you know the rules of bargaining! You may also note there are many books and magazines dedicated to this subject, just as there are in the postage stamp or coin collecting fields. One amulet in particular demand confers a 'thick skin,' that is, it fends off bullets and knife blades. Some people swear by its efficacy.

Tattoos

You may find that your driver's chest, back, or arms (as well as legs, hips, feet, and thighs, if you ever see them) are covered with tattoos. These may have been inscribed on his skin by the followers of a *rukkhadeva* (as described previously) or by a monk known for his knowledge of magic, or they may have been drawn on him in his village as a rite of passage. This is done when a young man is about 16 years old, so he must remember the pain he felt. Yet if you ask him about that, his chest will probably swell with pride.

City people who think they're very up-to-date have generally turned to amulets rather than the permanence of tattoos. The Thai government will not allow the employment in its service of men with too many obvious tattoos. These men are sometimes considered as low class or as having had a hillbilly upbringing.

Special Note on Buying Religious Paraphernalia
Many expats, as they get used to Thailand, find it of interest to buy religious items such as monks' bowls, Buddha images, sets of robes, or the ceremonial fans monks use when chanting. There are areas of Bangkok where these are made and sold. The only caution is that the government may not allow the export of what they suspect to be antiques without the proper paperwork from the Fine Arts Department. You also have to be careful about misuse of such items in an irreligious or disrespectful way. This even applies overseas, as particularly offensive incidents tend to get reported in Thai newspapers.

Don't use your monks' bowl as the dog's watering station; don't place Buddha images as doorstops; and, in Thailand at least, don't wrap yourself in the monks' robes to wow friends at a Halloween party.

It is also true that your delightful (and expensive) antiques may not be as old as you are, but if you enjoy them, fine. Just treat them with respect.

The Thai and I:
Understanding Your Hosts

The People Around You

During your stay in the kingdom, you are a foreigner. You also may be a *farang* by birth. You cannot change either situation. You might also keep in mind that being a foreigner who has come to Thailand to live and work makes you an expat. This word once indicated someone who had been exiled or banished.

What Thais Call Westerners

In Thai, a foreigner of whatever race is a *khon tangchat*. This means simply a 'person of another race, life, or birth.' If you are a Caucasian, no matter which country you come from, you are also a *farang*.

Farang, however, does not mean 'foreigner.'

The word *farang* has a long and interesting history, extending further back than the Crusades, to the Franks of Northern France. The Arabs and Turks who fought the invasions of Palestine called the Franks *ifrangi*, and the Persians picked it up as *farangi*. These Muslim cultures had extensive trade relations with Siam, and the term thus became known in the Far East.

Thai street children have had a lot of fun calling a passing *farang* a *farang khi nok*, a 'bird-dropping *farang*' after a guava of that name. This is seen by Thais as harmless, but it might annoy the *farang* if he or she understood it.

What Thais Call Others

Thais have identifying nicknames, not always polite, for those of other races or cultures. For example, two large groups present in Thailand are *khon cheen* (*jeen*) and *khon khaek*.

Cheen are the Chinese. Saying *khon cheen* makes it more polite. But there is a very common and less polite term, *chek*, which refers

to immigrant Chinese who came to Thailand to better themselves economically. They often started in lowly jobs, such as a pushcart peddler, but some went on to become millionaire capitalists. *Chek* are seen in a denigrating light and are regarded by some Thais as uncultured and uncouth. A rickshaw, for instance, used to be called a *rot chek*, a 'Chinaman's car.'

Khaek (literally 'guest') includes anyone who wears a turban, writes a language of right-to-left squiggles (Arabic, for instance), and who may well be Muslim, Sikh, or Hindu. This includes Indians, Pakistanis, Bangladeshis, Indonesians, Arabs of any country, Malays, and all Muslim Thais. Many Buddhist Thais will say a Muslim Thai citizen is a *khaek* and deny that that person is Thai until pressed on this point.

There are rude nicknames for a few other groups that Thais have identified: *Nikro*, Negro; *farang Asia*, Israelis or Turks or Iranians; and *Ai Yun*, Japanese, from their country's name in Thai, 'Yipun.'

Various hilltribe peoples are sometimes called *chao thai phu khao*, 'Thai people from the hills,' although they are generally looked down upon (except when the tourist authorities wish to promote them for Thailand's profit) and their legal status as citizens is always shaky.

Thais have no real awareness of Bulgars, Czechs, Poles, Lithuanians, and on and on, and therefore have no nicknames for them. They are all *farang*. Faced with a dark Paraguayan of Guarani descent or an American Indian, a Thai might call him 'Indian *daeng*' ('red Indian'), but that helps clarify very little. It would perhaps be best if you don't use any of these terms, other than *farang*, which has been accepted begrudgingly by Western foreigners as referring to them. The other terms almost certainly would be offensive to the groups involved.

Distinctions Between Thais

In the north of the kingdom you'll see Thais who tend to be of rather light skin colour and have eyes with the epicanthic fold we associate with the Chinese. As you travel to the deep south, near the Malaysian border, you'll find Thais with darker skin, big liquid black eyes, and sometimes the shorter, broader build of Malay stock. In big cities such as Bangkok, you may find the men taller than in rural districts, whether because of their diet or perhaps because the racial background is of a different mix. Young Thais tend to be taller and bigger than their grandparents. This is almost certainly the effect of improved nutrition, but nowadays, especially in the cities, it is also likely to be a result of Western junk food, which many wealthy kids are spoiled on.

Prejudice

Despite the wide range of racial and ethnic diversity amongst Thais, don't let anyone try to convince you there is no racial prejudice in Thailand. There is, and one thing it centres on is skin colour. In this, Thais are no different to many other cultures. Skin that is yellowish, dark, or a hue called *dam daeng*—a reddish tone of generally walnut colour—is often thought to be indicative of a peasant background. Parents may be much concerned about the skin tone of their daughters, for it affects their marriage prospects.

When I was a monk, there was some talk that Kenyans or Tanzanians might be coming to join the Order. Some Thais were quite upset at the prospect of black monks, but I thought they'd be striking in the saffron robes. Anyway, they didn't come. But it is unfortunately true that Africans

and other black people are thought by the Thais to be of a lower class than lighter-skinned people.

Some years ago, a popular joke went around: What is the best a Thai man can have to make him happy? The answer: a Chinese cook (many Thais enjoy Chinese cuisine), a Japanese wife (Japanese women have a good reputation for docility and attentiveness to their husbands), and a *farang* house (because such houses are reputed to be comfortable and well equipped). Someone tried to add a fourth, an American car, but the truth is that American cars are not popular for their size and lack of manoeuvrability in narrow lanes, and for their expensive operation and repairs.

There was another joke that also went around, but this was less innocent. If you're walking in the forest, carrying a walking staff and you encounter a snake, a tiger, and a *khaek*, which one do you beat first? The Thai answer is the *khaek*, which betrays the prejudice obviously.

Those termed *khaeks* are those people who keep to their own ways and therefore seem the least likely to assimilate with Thai culture. This may be off-putting to the Thais. This is especially true if you remember that jealousy is a prime cause of prejudice. And the truth is that many *khaek* people have come to Thailand, made it their home, and have done very well for themselves. So some Thais may resent this success. On the other hand, Chinese people started out with the same Thai prejudice against them, but have assimilated very well and 'have become Thai' more readily than *khaek* people.

Some Thais say of the Chinese in Thailand, "They work 25 hours a day, 32 days a month!" I don't understand why the Chinese aren't flattered by this, but they aren't. The Chinese may retort with, "Thais work flat on their backs."

Your Circle

It's possible that you came to Thailand alone and knew no one when you arrived. Or, you may have come with your family. It's also possible you already have a Thai person in your family. Perhaps you are a foreigner with a Thai spouse. Or one of your parents or step-parents is Thai. So let's talk about family first.

Having a Thai member of your family may prove a great asset to you in getting to know the country and learning the ways of its people. You, as an expat with a Thai spouse, will have someone to rely on who can take care of the myriad things that settling in requires—advice on where to live, getting a phone installed and electricity connected.

Your spouse, as with many Thai couples, may do a lot of the in-city driving. If you are a male employee and your Thai wife hasn't forgotten the Thai language, she can smooth the way for all your expat-Thai relationships, particularly in handling domestic staff, officials, and repairmen.

If your partner hails from the northeast (Isaan) and still speaks that language, he or she will prove invaluable in dealing with people from there. When it comes to hiring and firing, buying and selling, you're a lucky person. When it comes to your social life, however, you may not fare so well if your wife is originally from the servant class. There may be problems of acceptance into your world. In social situations, one often sees the men and the *farang* women gathered in one room and the Thai women in another. Some Thais may be more comfortable this way, particularly if the women have fewer language abilities.

On the other hand, it often happens that the husband's friends maybe unknown to the wife, and her friends may be strangers to her husband—particularly if he doesn't know enough Thai to get along.

If, as is happening more and more often, the *farang's* Thai wife comes from a higher class—educated and moneyed—that lady might feel less than happy at being relegated to socializing with other Thai women with whom she has little in common. Education, language, class—and always 'face'—may all be involved in this situation.

Invitations may prove to have awkward or distressing outcomes for expat-Thai relations, and may arise from *farang* wives who are used to giving dinner parties for their husbands' associates. Invitations for a business or working dinner in Thailand are usually extended to the employee and exclude the spouse. Social functions, on the other hand, generally include the spouse. Nowadays, decisions regarding whether or not to include spouses on invitations may be made according to the costs or expenses involved, not protocol. In some instances, while the invitation may not include a spouse, the invitee may nonetheless show up with a guest.

An even more serious difficulty the expat hostess may run into is the Thai who brings along more than one uninvited guest. As most Western food is served by the plate, and places are counted, it can be very disturbing if 12 people are invited and 16 come. This can happen. Or it would be disappointing to the hostess if she invited 12 people and only six showed up. Etiquette regarding responses to invitations is spotty at best. Most invitations now request a 'regrets only' response rather than an RSVP. Even so, most hosts and hostesses agree that a fifty percent response rate is good. Calling to confirm whether or not the invitee plans to attend is very common, whether the guest list is for ten or 100! The only solution for all of this is to relax, take it easy, expect the unexpected, be flexible, keep a cool heart (*chai yen*), and above all, smile.

Friends

If one parent is Thai and their children are then of mixed race (*luk khreung*), there will have to be some adjustments made. Thai kids are expected to be respectful of their parents and obedient (so far as it can be seen), and never, never talk back. Not all children play this part well if they've been raised in the US or other permissive societies where children enjoy a kind of independence that is seldom allowed a Thai child. Yet the Thai child, if you study the situation, may be far more independent in reality than the foreign one who boasts more about it.

For foreign kids to have Thai friends is, of course, a very good thing. But it may also be a situation that is dangerous, depending upon the kids, whether Thai, part-Thai, or expat. Although Thai and expat pre-schoolers may be playmates, once past school-entering age, there is a tendency for Thai and other children to separate. They have different needs and are under different kinds of stress. A Thai child in a Thai school is under pressure to conform, to study, to be polite, and to pass exams.

It's not quite the same for the expat children because they will be in a school that is less rigid than the Thai school. They may not have to wear a school uniform, which they may see in a very different light than the Thai student does. Western children often dislike uniforms. Thai children often wear theirs with pride, for not all can get into school and go on to university. Fewer Thai (than expat) students will stay with their education and successfully finish. To fail an exam may derail them; lack of money may deter them.

In contrast, many expat kids finishing high school will probably go on to university. Just at the critical juncture of finishing high school, Thai students are faced with fierce, kingdom-wide exams to finish school and again to get into the most desirable upper institutions. They may have to buckle down and study at special prep schools just as the expat kids are loosening up and having their school-ending proms and senior trips. This situation militates against expat-Thai friendships during school years, though it is true, many Thai university students get along very well with expats who are still in high school.

Attitudes Toward Sex

One problem with friends is that while a friendship may elevate one person, it may also do the opposite to the other. Drugs, drink, sexual

experimentation, sometimes crime, may arise from friendships that are ill-matched or perhaps too-well-matched on a low and descending level. Many Thai schoolboys experience sex at age 15 or 16, most often with a prostitute, attending upon her with a group of buddies. By age 17, most have become sexually experienced.

While the percentages of boys who have had sexual experience by age 17 may be similar amongst expats and Thai, the expat affairs are fewer with prostitutes than with girlfriends who are classmates.

This custom, by the way, is maintained by Thai men who work together. Inviting their expat colleague to go along can lead to domestic problems for him. Expat businessmen who travel with colleagues may sometimes run into a problem when they're included in their host's arrangements to visit a brothel after dinner. The expat bears the responsibility for finding a culturally appropriate way to handle these invitations. Practically every businessman will be faced with this dilemma, so it's best to plan ahead. This must be done in a way that will save everybody's face. One might say, 'I'm very tired,' or 'I'm too drunk and need to sleep.' If you know the colleague very well, you might more directly say, 'My culture deals differently with things like this, so I'm not going to join you.' Making a joke can also work, if it makes fun of nobody.

To illustrate the traditional Thai attitude that sex with prostitutes is just a form of recreation without much social backlash, let me tell a story. When I was a university lecturer, I was invited by my students to go on an overnight bus trip to act as chaperone. We loaded up our baggage, the tall drums and cymbals for the percussion band in the back of the bus, the other chaperones and students, male and female, and off we roared—chingkachang, chingkachung—into the late afternoon.

First stop: a gas station to fill up for the 600-kilometre journey. Second stop: a row of shops, upstairs of which was a busy brothel. Most of the boys leapt out with a loud cheer and made for the entrance. The rest of the boys, the girls, and the chaperones stayed behind on the bus, chatting till the business had been finished.

However, about half the boys clattered down the stairs and got on the bus rather glumly. It wasn't that they were so fast, it was that the brothelkeeper, upon seeing so many stalwart, hyped-up students, simply doubled the tariff to 100 baht. That was too rich for many of my students, who then re-boarded the bus and remained celibate along with the rest of us. All aboard, once again, we set off with a great cheer and banging from our *ching-chaap* band in the back, promptly forgetting about wayside brothels.

One thing that impressed me was that this all seemed so normal to everybody. Not to mention the ability of the young women to accept without complaint or comment on the shenanigans of their fellow classmates. Everything was simply accepted. A Thai would say, '*Mai pen rai.*'

If your friends are not merely "Thai fleas on the flank of a *farang*," as I've heard it put, you will find friendships quite close and helpful. One newspaper columnist reported that after some years here he had never made one Thai friend and was quite negative about the possibility of finding any. This is absurd. This person may have been interpreting the term 'friendship' in some narrow or peculiar way.

In fact, although Thais do not become emotionally intimate in the same way as some Westerners do, they are a warm and gregarious people. Once you get to know them, they are as good a friend as any other. You may well have to make the first move, but once it's made, so is the friendship.

Thais, like some other groups, do not entertain much at home. Wealthy Thais may prefer hotel settings or large and fancy restaurants, though there are those who do cater dinner in for their guests. You may, however, receive an invitation from a Thai friend to visit his parent's home or to go to his village for a weekend, not uncommon among simpler people who may like you and not feel they have to pretend to be wealthy.

When you are introduced to your friend's parents or grandparents, show every respect to them, *wai*ing and accepting whatever goodie or drink is offered you. Thais may 'know' you are fearful of Thai food and of the water, so when you're offered a Coke, unopened, in a dust-covered bottle with no ice, say 'Thank you' and smile.

Take a sip if you wish, and set it to one side. The offer is considered polite and hospitable, but no one requires you to drink it. And be sure to rave over the rare beauty and cleverness of a grandchild just as you would anywhere else in the world. You may well be a hit with that friend's family, which is all to the good.

Domestic Staff and Their Thai Traits

The purpose of talking about domestic staff here is that many expats' first exposure to Thais and Thai culture is through relating to their domestic staff. A household full of expats can learn a lot from them. If you can find a language to communicate in, besides that of giving a half-dozen commands, your domestic staff might have wonderful tales to tell about their earlier lives, their families, their homes, and lots more. They might even be able to show you some of the tricks of the domestic's trade: Thai cooking, for instance, and how to go to a market other than the air-conditioned supermarket you'd feel more at home in.

Domestic staff can take care of your children when you're out, if they are trained for it. Some are terrific with expat kids, and some are completely inexperienced. Just remember that your kids may be able to get your maids to remain silent, or 'forget' certain details, or even tell mild lies.

"Noi, what time did Tommy come in last night?" asks an expat mother who'd gone off to some social function the night before.

"Oh, madam, Tommy not late. Not too late."

"Was he alone? Had he been drinking?"

"Tommy, he come alone. Not drinking, too."

"Are you quite sure?"

"Very sure. Noi not see."

'Noi not see' can cover a lot of territory!

One should not underestimate the Thais' capacity for fun. You can probably get your domestic staff to do the most unpleasant of jobs for enough money, but if that lousy job could be made fun, too, perhaps he'd do it for free . . . especially if you throw in a bottle of whiskey for good measure.

Domestic helpers, like many other Thais, if they know anything at all about your country, have learned it from the television. This means they know hardly anything accurate at all.

"*Nai* ('Master'), do your papa and mama live there?" asked a maid I once employed, pointing to a newspaper picture of the Empire State Building in Manhattan.

"No, not quite," I answered. I searched for a photo of my family home—a single-storey wooden house surrounded by plants and trees, a wide double garage door in the front wall, and wider lawns around the house. Proudly, I announced, "Isn't it nice?"

The maid smiled slightly, but her disappointment couldn't be hidden. *Nai* must be some kind of farmer, she must have thought. Real expats from that country live in skyscrapers, right?

"*Nai*, how many buffalo your father have?" she then asked.

"None," I said. "We don't have water buffaloes in America."

"Oh, but *Nai* do. Saw in movie about Indian *daeng*."

"Well, yes, but buffalo in America are not the same as the Thai *khwai*."

"Yes."

"No not same."

"Yes."

It became a 'Yes, we have no bananas' syndrome.

"Yes," I said.

"Yes do?"

"Have no. Maybe tomorrow."

On occasion, after asking your permission (or perhaps even before asking), the cook may receive visitors—her mother and some aunties and assorted nieces and nephews and cousins. They may have come to Bangkok to visit someone in a hospital, and have been put up in your cook's room—all of them. Feeling generous and kindly, you invite them for dinner.

"Oh, no, madam. No can do," your cook tells you. "Eat in room better."

"We'll have Thai food for them. For all of us. Do invite them," the kind expat insists.

You can wait until Thailand has glaciers, but they won't come to dinner in your dining room. And they shouldn't. On the other hand, an offer to use a table or mat out in the garden or on a balcony outside where they can have their own meal together, out of your way, might be gratefully accepted.

Why this rejection of your kind invitation to dine at your table? You've just had your first real lesson in the hierarchical structure of Thai society and the rules of status each Thai knows by heart. You must learn them, as well.

Les Miserables

While fewer and less miserable than in certain other lands, in Thailand there are beggars and sick people on the street. Drop them a coin if you wish; it's considered meritorious for people of all religions. Also be advised sometimes that these unfortunates are 'working' a route or a corner for a gang boss. If you watch long enough, you may see a car come near the beggar and someone step out to pick up the beggar, whisking him or her away, leaving behind a replacement. The next shift, so to speak.

Blind singers and instrumentalists often occupy a wide spot near the road. Give to them if you wish, it's also meritorious—except to the municipal authorities, who'll complain that you're encouraging begging by helping to make it pay.

No matter how sorry you may feel for a particular beggar, having to sit all day in rags, breathing the polluted roadside air, do not invite him home for a bath and a meal. This might prove foolhardy and dangerous.

I Swear to Tell the Half-Truth

Depending upon how rigid you are, one characteristic of many Thais is their seeming inability to tell the whole, unvarnished truth. Often I've found myself the butt of a creative deception, and many times when I could see no need for it.

Once, when I was supervising an examination at the university, I caught a student apparently receiving answers from someone just out of my sight, beyond the open door. I quietly left my post near the front of the room and approached the student's desk. I was right, beyond a shadow of a doubt: he was attempting to receive an answer from someone just outside. That person saw me first, made a signal, and disappeared. The student, unaware I was standing practically over him, made as if to call his friend back, and was startled when I removed the exam paper from the top of his desk, impounding it. He sat there glumly until the end bell and then disappeared.

A day or so later, the dean sent for me. "Achaan Roger, perhaps you should take the week off. Go home and don't come back to your classes for a week. Mr. So-and-so was very angry that you caught him."

I did take the week off and, at home, I peeked out the gate before I stepped into the lane in front of my house. I never did see Mr. So-and-so again, but I heard about the case from several teachers and friends.

'You were lucky he didn't seek revenge in some way' was the gist of their comments.

I asked a Thai friend about this. He did not seem to share my concern that the student had been cheating, and I had, alone, it appeared, stood up for the sanctity of examinations. "What should I have done?" I wheedled.

"Why did you see it?" my friend asked.

"See what?" I asked.

"See the student cheating."

"That was my job. I was supervising to prevent cheating."

"Yes, yes," he said. "I understand. But why did you see him?"

He explained these possible scenarios:

Maybe it was the student's last term, and now he wouldn't graduate. Maybe he comes from a large, poor family. They are all sacrificing to send him to the university and waiting for him to graduate and get a good job so he could send his *nong* ('younger' brother or sister) to study next. When that one had graduated, then the two of them could send No. 3 to school . . . until all the family's offspring had been awarded their degrees and were set up with good jobs. This way the whole family could get a leg upward on financial security and all would benefit.

And I possibly had spoiled it by looking and seeing this one student getting help from outside the room. My pleas that I was doing my duty met with short shrift. It cost me nothing to let the boy quietly pass, but could cost his family dearly. And as for the cheating, had I caught everyone who was peeking surreptitiously at notes or copying from someone else? I had happened to see just this one and, by my rigidity, had perhaps consigned his family to continuing poverty. *I was the villain* of the piece.

153

The opposite could have also been true and I remain the villain. The student could have been the favoured scion of a rich and powerful family. To cause him to lose face could have turned out worse for me than for him.

There is a way of avoiding problems—though it's hardly limited to the Thais—and that is to give a false name or fake phone number with people you just meet. I found I felt better sometimes if I used an acronym of my name: George. And by happy chance, few Thais can pronounce George. They manage to get out *yoo* or *yawt*, which means 'top,' 'summit,' or 'peak.' That was all right with me, and so for years Yod was my name.

When I asked another friend about this tendency of some Thais to give false names or say they worked elsewhere than they really did, my friend said, "Why should I tell the truth to anyone who asks? I don't know why he wants to know, do I? And it doesn't make any difference, does it?"

I had a problem (as I saw it) with Thais who asked my nationality—US—or assumed it and then thought I must like Coca-Cola. I don't happen to like Coca-Cola nor a number of other things they thought any *real* American ought to like. When I consulted a Thai friend, his advice was to say I'm from somewhere else.

"But I am an American," I replied.

"He doesn't have to know."

Is that cheating, or is it simply preserving my independence? As for my address, I give my post office box or answer that I live in Soi Santisuk. An article on addresses in the *Bangkok Post* I once read stated there were 12 *sois* ('lanes') by that name in Bangkok, so I felt that should adequately cover my trail from casual acquaintances. As for the phone number, either I could say I had none, or again just trim the truth a bit. If it's been raining heavily, my phone won't work for a few days. That's the same as having no phone, right?

Am I lying? No, I am being properly intercultural, acting like several of my Thai friends. I am smoothing social relationships, perhaps saving face for myself or somebody else.

Misconceptions

It may take you a little while to become aware that most Thais don't know a whole lot about expats. But you will find that they may know more about you than the average person in your country knows about Thailand.

"Have you ever seen cow playing?" I was once asked by a Thai who knew I had lived in Spain and Mexico for several years.

I didn't get it, but you may have. 'Cow playing' is bullfighting.

The only other thing my Thai friends 'knew' of Spain was that all Spaniards were romantic and strummed guitars to show it.

The first and most basic misconception Thai people have is that expats are all rich. Even the baggy shorts, sandal-shod backpacker may have a camera and American Express cheques in his rucksack. Even dressed like coolies, we are—to many simple Thai—rich beyond belief. They arrive at this conclusion if only by virtue of our having been able to travel here at all.

Other generalizations and misconceptions commonly held by Thai people are:

Farangs like to travel alone (but Thais find their fun in groups);

Farangs live exclusively on pizza, hamburgers, and bread for every meal;

Thai women and *farang* men fall in love easily because Thai women are taught to be polite and unassuming and helpful, while *farang* men are usually brought up to be polite and gentle to women;

Americans, Australians, and Germans are big and loud-mouthed;

Brits have sharp noses and narrow nostrils (which are highly regarded by the more flat-nosed Thais);

The French are stand-offish;

All *farangs* are honest and can be used as reliable witnesses at the police station. (No one seems yet to have heard of robbery or murder of taxi drivers in *farang*land.);

Farangs cannot eat spicy Thai food.

Thais of higher class—richer, better educated, and Westernized—may find these misconceptions off-putting. Let them stand as the exceptions, while the misconceptions are those of the more modest classes who haven't had a chance to go abroad to shop, visit, or study.

Hand and Body Language

As soon as the chance presents itself for you to participate in a cross-cultural workshop, do make an effort to attend. There is a lifetime of learning to be had there, plus some mistakes to avoid. Some faux pas can be seriously inhibitive of good intercultural relationships. Expats often give signals that can be offensive to Thais, or simply not understood, or the other way around, too.

How we sit, stand, move, gesture, and speak may become a bombshell in our ongoing daily lives. How do you call a waiter's attention in a restaurant? Hiss like a displeased cobra, as in Spain? You'll not only get the attention of your waiter, but the attention of all the other diners, and no one will flash a friendly smile at you.

Take a trip on a *khlong* boat and see how Thais wave hello at you. They hold their palm out, flapping their hand left and right, or right and left, at the end of their wrist, their arm turning back and forth as if on an axis.

Try smiling as if you don't really mean it. It's been said that Thais use 16 or so different smiles for different purposes. Maybe so, but some are called 'dry smiles' and aren't meant in love or friendship. It would be good to learn some of the different nuances.

Warning!

Don't pat anyone on the head with your hand or with anything else. Patting on the head is impolite, unless it is a small child or you are close to someone as in family members, friends, or a partner.

Don't point at people and things with your feet, and don't shunt things aside with them. Feet are for walking on and for aching if you've been out on them all day. Don't call needless attention to your corns or bunions, and if you have to refer to your feet or legs, always precede it with 'Excuse me.'

Don't speak loudly or shout. It will definitely prove better to scold and reprimand in private. Unless your Thai is very good, don't try sarcasm. It doesn't work well amongst Thais even if they understand it.

Don't criticize everything under the Thai sun. Remember, if you're upset at corruption or criminality here, just think of Chicago in the violin-case days. Not everyone is as aware as you. Of course, they may be, but are just keeping their cool about it. Complain about traffic if you wish, but you'll bore your listeners just as the traffic bores you. People might start singing a line or two from a popular song, "*Buea khon bon*" . . . "I'm bored with grumblers."

Don't offer money and other things with the *left* hand. The left is mainly reserved for other bodily functions.

Don't expect your Muslim domestic staff to wash your pet dog. It's against their religion.

And finally, *don't* fail to learn as much as you can as quickly as you can. This way you'll enjoy life here more fully.

Social Values

There are certain values a society maintains that, when taken as a whole, give that society a colouration unlike any other. There may be similarities, however, among examples in the same 'family' groups. East Asians, for instance, based their writing system upon Chinese. Japan, Korea, and

Vietnam all used variations based on it in their literary or legal works. These countries form a 'family' in writing, religion, and political and social forms.

The 'Indo' part of Indochina is a name reflective of another language system and is composed of those countries that use an Indian alphabet with local variations. These are Burma, Thailand, Laos, Cambodia, and the Mon people who live in today's Burma and Thailand.

Bangladesh, Tibet, Nepal, Bhutan, Java, and Bali emphasize the 'Indo' part more than Thailand does. The ancient Thai religious systems, as well as the forms of monarchy and law throughout the region, are clearly of Indian origin.

Hierarchies

The American Declaration of Independence is dedicated to the idea that all men [people] are created equal. This is not the case in Thailand. From the lowest beggar on the street to His Majesty the king and His Holiness the supreme patriarch, each and every Thai has a well-delineated place in relation to every other Thai. The king and the patriarch stand at the summit; some are at the very bottom. In between are various social levels, and every Thai knows how to determine their status in relation to everyone else. This shows them how to behave in relation to everyone else, too. Thailand is a country where everything is determined by one's status in relation to everyone else's. Non-Thais need to learn the basics of determining the status of Thais they relate with, as well as determining their own place in the hierarchy. Thais will be doing the same in relation to you. This is not 'democratic,' but it helps you (and all Thais) to interact smoothly and consistently.

Let's look at some Thai ways of determining status, and the hierarchies non-Thais will likely need to know about. Technically, the *Sangharaja* and every other monk out-ranks anybody else. But Thailand is a kingdom where, in law and custom, the king, an 'attribute' of the god Vishnu, is conceded the highest place amongst *all the people*. Here is the order of ranking royalty:

HM—His Majesty the King;

HM—Her Majesty the Queen;

159

HRH—His/Her Royal Highness (members of the immediate royal family).

Descendants of kings:

Somdej Chao Fa—child of a king by a royal mother;

Phra Ong Chao—child of a king not by a royal mother; nowadays always the grandchild of a king;

MC—*Mom Chao*, the grandchild of a king, but not in line of succession;

MR—*Mom Rajavong*, the great-grandchild of a king;

ML—*Mom Luang*, the great-great-grandchild of a king.

After the fifth generation, the bearer reverts to being a commoner. Thailand once had a very extensive royal family; if there had been no way to 'reduce' the titled people back to commoner status, by now every garland seller and boat driver might have a title of some sort. This way, with each generation (except in the immediate succession) the royals drop down a rank and eventually become plain Nai and Nang, Mr. and Mrs., but they are entitled to use *na Ayudhya* after their surnames.

As complicated as this system may appear, it is far simpler than a century ago. Except for His Majesty the King, Thailand has no perpetually hereditary titles. At one time there were many princes 'of here' or 'of there,' but the territorial titles have all been abolished, as have life peerages. Or they have been allowed to lapse as the former holders died off. Thailand today has no equivalent of dukes, earls, barons, and the like.

In the Buddhist Monks' Order

All Buddhist monks are called *bhikkhu*, as discussed previously. All monks together make up the *Sangha*, the Buddhist monkhood or Order. Of course, as the monks are celibate, there can be no question of inheriting rank or title. When a monk dies or leaves the Order (disrobes), his rank as a monk vanishes.

Aside from the Buddha himself, who claimed to be a *bhikkhu* like all his followers, the following ranks have come into being within the hierarchy:

Sangharaja—head of the Buddhist monkhood in a given country;

Somdej—a role much like a Catholic cardinal (a 'prince');

Mahâthera—a monk in the Order for twenty years;

Thera—a monk of ten years in the Order;

Navaka—(pronounced in Thai nawaka), less than five years as a monk;

Samanera—a novice monk, not fully ordained;

Upasaka—a devout layman keeping the eight precepts;

Upasika—a devout laywoman keeping the same eight precepts, often called a 'nun' or, in Thai, *mae chi*.

There are also other titles that are dependent upon the monk's position. As a teacher, he might be called *phra khru* (*khru* is the same as 'guru,' an Indian term that has become intelligible and popular in the West; it means 'teacher'). Also *chao khun* ('ecclesiastical governor'), *chao khana changwat* ('ecclesiastical governor of a province'); *chao khana tambon* ('ecclesiastical governor of a smaller district'); and chao arwat ('abbot' of a monastery or *wat*).

Social Virtues Adopted by Thais from Buddhism

Buddhist-inspired virtues that are basic to the well-developed and healthy, socialized person, in the Thai view, are:

Dâna. 'Generosity.' You will see this practiced in many ways: gifts given to and by social superiors, donations to charities, and so on. If you study the matter you will find that *dâna* is not considered meritorious if you give with strings or conditions attached. You know a down-and-outer and you offer him money saying, 'This is for a pair of shoes. It is not to be wasted on drink!' This is a 'gift,' but it has been conditioned by the restriction of not buying a drink, so it isn't technically *dâna.*

Sîla. 'Morality.' Being a morally upright and ethical person is a universal value in all cultures. But culture determines the definition. For example, do not kill. Why? Because to go through your life with hostility toward others (any others) is not a desirable way of behaving, and cancels out loving kindness. In some cultures, this would ban hunting and fishing as well as making war. Or, in others, it means you should not destroy the environment upon which others depend. A lack of morality (and this is only the first clause) will prevent you from developing a sensitive and generous love for all fellow creatures. The study of what Thais consider moral, and then a comparative search for your own cultural values on this subject, is a rich one indeed, and will teach you as much about yourself as it will about the Thais.

Bhâvanâ. 'Spiritual and mental development.' To many Thais this is the goal of life: clear-mindedness, the ability to penetrate the truth of our human condition, and to purify our actions so we can develop our sensitivity and understanding. Many Thais think that this quality can be attained by intensive meditation; many more think it means being the best Buddhist one can be—praying, paying respect to religious images and monks, and all those ritualistic behaviours that make merit for oneself and others

Web of Responsibility

Of other social values traditionally held important in Thailand, one is the 'web of responsibility' that Thai people generally go by. These responsibilities include: your king—to respect him and obey his laws; your parents—to obey them, pay respect and care for them; your brothers, sisters, and other relatives—to protect them; your children—such as your responsibility to see they marry well, to provide proper wives for your sons for the benefit of them and the family; your employees and, in past times, your slaves—to take care of them; your teachers—to respect and protect them and to obey their teachings.

This web of social obligation and responsibilities is taught everywhere in Thailand—at home, in school, in the media, seemingly in the very air the Thais breathe.

Phi-Nong

One of the most easily observed of Thai social values is embodied in so-called *phi-nong* relationships, those between elders, *phi*, and younger people, *nong*. These two words can be translated as 'elder brother' or 'elder sister,' and 'younger brother' and 'younger sister,' but they do not require people to be related. In a school, for instance, the members of the senior class are *phi* to the members of the junior class. In a working situation, the *phi* is the elder to the younger worker. It is fun to listen to and watch two Thais, who have just met, probe about in an attempt to determine who is who.

The *phi* deserves respect, protection of his reputation, obedience, and respectful service. The *nong* deserves protection and to be advised and cared for by his *phi*. This is very important in Thai culture. Although obedience may not mean always and forever doing services and following instructions, it is not acceptable for a *nong* to flout the elder's instructions or advice by ignoring them. Nor will you hear in Thailand, when a *phi* asks a *nong* to fetch him a Coke, 'Get it yourself.' This expression of attitude would shock a lot of Thais.

This type of relationship may occur between boss and employee, teacher and pupil, *bhikkhu* and novice or *dek wat* (a boy who lives in the temple), husband (always the *phi* in the house, regardless of true ages) and wife, and so on.

Expats sometimes treat lower status Thais too 'highly' and high status Thais too 'normally,' both of which can get the *farang* in trouble at home, work, or with friends. So learn how to tell the differences in status between yourself and everyone else, and learn who are your *phi* and who are your *nong*.

Group-Oriented

I originally came to Thailand from Spain by a combination of walking, hitchhiking, bicycling, and riding trains, buses, and ships. When I reached Thailand, people would ask, "How many were travelling in your group?" When I answered, "Just me, alone," they would look puzzled and then dismiss my way of travel with "*Mai sanuk*"—'not fun.' Thais don't consider being alone, or doing things alone, as acceptable fun or even normal behaviour. For one thing, there's no real Thai word for 'privacy' and certainly no concept that a person might just enjoy solitary peace and quiet in a beautiful place or at home. No Thai would ever say, like Greta Garbo, "All I want is to be left alone!"

Every Thai will have his own secrets or dreams he may not share with anyone, but keep in mind that, as a rule, there are no secrets for long in Thailand. This may seem to contradict what was just said about the importance of the group and the strangeness of the concept of privacy. But think of it this way: a Thai's privacy is internal, where a Westerner's may be external and physical. Thais are group-oriented and private within themselves at the same time.

Mai Pen Rai

". . . Grant me the serenity to accept the things I cannot change. . . ."

This portion of the Alcoholics Anonymous "Serenity prayer" is certainly believed and acted upon by many Thais. How deep the serenity may go when a student has just flunked out of his university because of having failed a key course, or when your long-awaited new car is crumpled up by a ten-wheel truck, or you fail to get hired for the job you've been hankering for, I don't know. But the Thais I have known certainly deserve the *Tukkata Thong* (the 'Golden Doll' equivalent to an Oscar) if they're merely play-acting that they're not disappointed. I think the truth is that they may feel disappointed, but they're going to accept it and move on. *Mai pen rai*!

The title of a book of her experiences in Thailand by the late Carol Hollinger—and a very funny book it is—*Mai Pen Rai Means Never Mind* is based on the Thai expression that is usually translated as such. It's what you say when the landlady's representative tries to explain why the repairman has not yet come and it's only ten days since he promised to. It's a 'you're welcome' when someone thanks you for a gift. It's a common expression that will defuse most situations that have a bit of tension in them. It doesn't mean you don't care, but if there's nothing to be done about a situation, use it at least as an opener and to get everyone off the hook:

"Oh, you'll have to excuse the postman. He dropped the letters in a puddle when he slipped on the steps. Here they are, a bit damp."
"*Mai pen rai.* They'll dry out in front of a fan."

"I'm so sorry I'm late for our meeting. The traffic is terrible."
"*Mai pen rai.* No one can beat the traffic."

"My secretary was sick today, so she hasn't typed our contract yet."
"*Mai pen rai.* Tomorrow will be soon enough."

Mai pen rai is not necessarily a cop-out or an indication of your disinterest, but rather it simply means that you're not going to get all worked up at this moment. Of course, you couldn't use it to anyone in response to the announcement of a parent's death. In this situation it would show a cold-heartedness that would repel everyone, even a very detached, unemotional person. But for lesser matters, particularly things that have happened already and that you couldn't prevent, it's adequate as a short, immediate response. Expats should learn to use it, and learn to accept it.

I recommend Carol Hollinger's book for some happy reading of Thailand as it was nearly forty years ago. Despite the subsequent development, you may recognize the place and the people and get a good idea why so many expats before you fell in love with the country, its people, and their ways.

If you can find it, also acquire a copy of W.A.R. Wood's collection of short stories, *Consul in Paradise*, which deals with the period from just before the end of the nineteenth century to the 1950s, or so.

These two books, Hollinger's and Wood's, give an excellent and amusing introduction to the Thailand and Siam that was, and how others before you learned to work and live amongst the Thais.

The whole concept of *mai pen rai* strikes me as pretty healthy. By comparison, I was once standing outside a hospital in Palermo, Italy, when a local man rushed out, threw himself over a car, and began to beat it, wailing and carrying on something terrible. I assumed that his beloved wife had just died in childbirth—what else could warrant such a display of wild emotion? But no. No wife or baby died. He had merely locked his car keys in the car and had no spare. That's all. No *mai pen rai* there.

Co-operation

Until the emergence of the economic forces that are re-making Thailand, 'competition' was something of a dirty word. Buddhist teachings downplay ambition as unwholesome and producing pain and unhappiness. The Buddha taught kinder, gentler values, particularly those that lead to satisfaction rather than to dissatisfaction. It is interesting to note how the international Outward Bound schools teach co-operation. No group of students get credit until all members of the group have passed the test, be it scaling a wall or rappelling down a cliff face. Instead of hailing a few star performers, the entire team can smile at the successful result of their total effort. That is what is meant in Thai philosophy by co-operation. Even though Thai people are competitive, even intensely so sometimes, there is this rich vein of co-operation that connects everybody. Again, reconciling this seemingly contradictory state of affairs is a fascinating study.

Seniority

This is a concept known worldwide, although today it is being discarded in some places as an impediment to economic development. Some old geezer holds the job till he dies or retires. He will not be thrown out for some bright-eyed and eager young cub coming up the line of promotion. This produces a great and unchanging social calm until the ambitious young one forces a change, chases out the elders, and takes their place.

The seniority system is safer and more socially stable since everyone knows where he or she stands. But one must be patient and wait for the old fogeys to move on. It was dissatisfaction with waiting for a turn at power that caused the young, French-educated bureaucrats and military men to conspire to overthrow King Rama VII and his uncles in 1932.

The power of seniority, in Thai called *avuso*, is still quite common in the government, military, civil service, and in businesses. To throw established elders out of their positions of rank and power into 'inactive posts' is one way of disempowering them, keeping them satisfied or at least quiet, and preserving their face.

Now that the value of elders is diminished somewhat by modern theories, there remains a problem of how to keep them out of mischief. Retirement with honours is one way that is less dangerous to the interests of new power groups than to simply toss them out of their offices. This explains the delicacy with which the Thai government handles traitors in the military who have staged unsuccessful coups, such as the one in 1991. No Thai government can afford to arouse the enmity of the military establishment.

In an attempted coup in the mid-1980s, an intra-military struggle found its dénouement in the murder-execution of one of the generals. This kind of outcome is rare in Thai politics because the seniority system and its stability have value. Even though ideas are changing in this area, it is not wise to ignore seniority in any social and professional setting in Thailand.

Accepting Authority

Closely tied to the hierarchical attitudes of Thai society, these further concepts of group-orientation, seniority, and the acceptance of authority tie together well. Many a businessman has discovered that to schedule a meeting of his employees may produce nothing of initiative, innovation, or frankness. Everyone waits for the boss to tell them what to do, think, or say. There is an atmosphere of acceptance ('Whatever you say, boss!') till the businessman feels he's surrounded by spongy matter, not people with ideas and drive.

Thais are taught that accepting authority is the mark of a polite person. Self-starting or assertive behaviour is seen as rude or aggressive. This causes a lot of problems in all sectors: at home with the maid, at work with Thai managers, or with your friends.

I once taught an English course at the largest Thai bank. I must confess my students sure taught *me* a lesson in Thai culture and behaviour. To stir up conversation I went around the room asking my students, "What do you think of General de Gaulle as president of France?"

I got absolutely nowhere, and very fast at that. Not a single student, all university graduates holding down good jobs at the bank, had any opinion of de Gaulle, who was big in the newspapers at that time. Not one of them stated approval or disapproval. It was as if no one had ever heard of de Gaulle.

One of the students, an unusually assertive young man—meaning that he'd dare to express an answer at least—asked me in turn, "Why should I have an opinion about General de Gaulle?" That stopped me then, and it stops me now. Why indeed, must we have an opinion on General de Gaulle? Or on so many other matters that clutter our minds and memories? How often is it that our opinion is merely that of our grandfather? Or of our teachers? This young man was expressing the beginnings of thinking for himself rather than just waiting to be told what to think. But authoritarian views are still more common here in Thailand. Thus, many liberation movements are alien here, although recently there are some signs that more free-thinking ideas are coming.

Another learning experience I had at the bank was the effect on the class of a fellow student of rank. Every once in a while, the president-founder's secretary would sit in. Though she was a student, she was very busy and her duties took precedence over mere English study, so she played hooky quite often. When she came, the class was not the pleasant, relaxed group it usually was. She had an inhibiting affect that killed spontaneity. The reason for this was that, by comparison, she was of higher status than all of the others. Thus, she had more authority—even more than the teacher. She was impressive in her manner, what I'd term formidable.

Still, I tried to act the teacher. I asked the class to catch the error in an intentionally incorrect sentence, or to define a word. Once she had spoken, it was amazing how everyone else came up with the same answer, even our more assertive young man. Even when her answer was wrong, no one dared say so by correcting the exercise. It was awe-inspiring and I could see why expat businessmen in Thailand sometimes fail to adjust to working with Thais. This makes training for working in a cross-cultural setting so essential.

Luckily, a few companies offer such training. Unfortunately, many firms do not. And so the Western executive, who may have enjoyed huge success back home, totally fails to adjust to realities here and may have to be relocated elsewhere. This represents a great expense to a company and to all the people involved, both financially and emotionally.

Saving Face

Connected to all this is the concept of 'face' and the massive effort (natural to Thais and most other Asians, but hard to learn for expats) to save both yours and others. To have corrected the lady-secretary in public would have meant a massive loss of face for her amongst her juniors in the bank. No one would ever correct her. Everyone would recognize the situation and work to save her face by not mentioning it. Had anyone done otherwise, it might have served to sever his relationship to the bank. If I had done it, it would have endangered my job, too!

Everywhere in Thailand—in government, the military, in the monkhood, in academe, at home, with friends, and in business—saving face is supreme. The government has the previously mentioned inactive posts to save the face of someone who, in another society, might be fired, made to resign, or jailed. In Thailand, he is shunted to a position where he cannot repeat his mistake, because he will have no authority to make damaging decisions. This is done despite whatever efficiency must be sacrificed. Sudden re-assignment is usually a sign that someone has boo-booed, but no one wants to say it outright. An inspection trip to Europe or America may be the equivalent of the inactive post, a sort of golden banishment. It gives the public time to forget whatever the infamy was.

Thais have a remarkable ability to forget for face-saving purposes. The Thai newspapers may rage about someone's fallibility, anything from corruption to murder, and within weeks it has totally disappeared from the public consciousness. Then, when the matter seems to have blown over, when that same miscreant is named for something equally bad, no one seems to recall that he is a second-time bounder.

Well, it reduces the temperature for a while. That's the purpose of face-saving, anyhow.

Individual Values

There are, of course, many other values that govern a Thai's behaviour toward others. To some extent, these co-ordinate with the overall social values already explained. Some of the most important of these values are discussed here. The subheading is the Romanized spelling of the Thai word.

Kreng Chai (Often Written as 'Jai')

Literally, this term means 'considerate,' 'unassuming,' unwilling to push oneself onto others or to cause inconvenience to status superiors. It means staying intentionally in the background or not putting oneself forward. *Kreng chai* is always applied by status inferiors toward those of superior status. A son would be *kreng chai* of his father and not ask for pocket money. An employee would be *kreng chai* of his employer and not ask for an extra day off. The employee or father will not be *kreng chai* toward sons or employees, but must show sympathy (*hen chai*) to them.

Hai Kiat

Giving honour, dignity, and respect, such as attending a wedding. You may be asked to say a few words or give a blessing to the couple. You might even be asked by the MC to sing. Other ways of being respectful or giving someone honour or dignity can cross cultural barriers very readily. So use common sense in this area. Remember, this is a society that is very proud and sensitive to perceived slights, so bending over backward to give respect is a good idea. This is true even in relation to status inferiors.

You will be seen as a very honourable person if you learn to give respect (and therefore face) to status inferiors while maintaining your own status and remaining aware of your own place in the social hierarchy, as well. This is a fascinating area for further study. The longer you stay in Thailand, the more subtle will be the cues you are able to discern in how face and status and *hai kiat* all mesh to work together in this society.

Nam Chai (Literally 'Water of the Heart')

Extending generosity without expecting anything in return for it.

Saksri

This concept concerns dignity, self-image, and self-esteem. Once again, it includes both oneself and relationships with others. Becoming boisterous in a bar or putting people in a position of ridicule is hardly guarding one's own *saksri,* or that of another person.

Hen Chai (Literally 'To See the Heart')

'Sympathetic understanding,' perhaps of a person in trouble or one unable to do what he wants and needs, or what you want or need him to do. Your secretary, in a hurry to get home to tend a sick child, makes a mistake in a letter she's typed. Do you insist she stay late to re-type it? Or do you say, 'Never mind, I'll correct it by pen and send it off.' *Mai pen rai* may lead to sloppiness when letting people off the hook, but it is also forgiving of a minor error.

Chai Yen (Literally 'Cool Heart')

A 'cool mind,' not 'cold-heartedness.' One of the worst flaws anyone can reveal in Thailand is to become 'hot-hearted,' visibly angry or ill-tempered, and, by the Thai definition, out of control. To become angry is *moho*. In common Thai parlance it also carries connotations of 'madness.' To lose your cool is regarded as a form of temporary insanity, and people will avoid you rather than try to deal with you and whatever the problem may have been in the first place. This virtue of 'keeping cool, being patient' is the one most inculcated amongst Thais and most often found lacking in expats. You may have learned to be assertive and direct, but Thais are also telling you that if you show your anger, you lose face and are considered out of control. The rule is: the angrier you are, the more you smile. That is a tough one for Westerners to adapt themselves to.

Chai Rawn (Literally 'Hot Heart')

This is the opposite of 'cool mind' and is not at all respected in Thailand. Whatever the cause, don't become 'hot-hearted.' Keep your dignity (or *hai kiat*), don't shout and turn red—an apt description of the out-of-control expat. From a Thai point of view, there is no justification for allowing this emotion full play. If a Thai shows anger this visibly, something has gone drastically wrong. Mayhem may not be far away. Unless, of course, the Thai has been Westernized by living abroad and has the same problem adjusting to Thai values as you did when you first arrived.

Moh Som

This term is translated as 'appropriate,' 'suitable,' 'fitting.' Again, older Thais find great value in being *moh som*. This includes the way one dresses, speaks, moves, and talks. Attending a funeral in jeans and a T-shirt is not *moh som*. Nor is chewing gum, combing your hair, or licking an ice cream cone as you walk along the street. Women in particular, but not alone, used to face many rules—and not only Thai women, but just about all women—that were intended to preserve their dignity or femininity. Whatever one called it, that was close to the Thai *moh som*.

Another aspect of *moh som* is that of body modesty. Topless or nude sunbathing at beaches is not *moh som*! Consider the following story:

A young European educator flew into Bangkok to take up his contract teaching his language to Thai university students. He was welcomed by his Thai colleagues-to-be and taken to a large house on the beach. He was assigned a room there and told about meal hours. His host told him to make himself comfortable, unpack, enjoy a bath, and then come down for dinner.

As he had always done, our European lecturer took off his clothes after he'd stepped into the bathroom, which was a large, tiled room with a number of showerheads around the walls. He neatly piled everything on a shelf near the door, walked to a convenient shower, and turned on the water. Squeezing some of his shampoo out of its tube, he worked it into his hair. A great fuzz of lather coursed down his face, blinding him. But he found it a great relief after 14 hours on a non-stop flight. He groped on the floor for the bar of soap that had escaped his grasp, scooting it across the floor, and as he fumbled about, the shower washed the suds from his eyes. At that same moment, he opened one eye to look for the soap . . . and discerned a bare foot.

Standing up, he passed his hands over his face and looked about. To his surprise, there were now several other men in the bathroom, each busily soaping or rinsing or shampooing, and all of them staring at him. It immediately registered on him that all the others were wrapped in some kind of colourful cloth; he realized with a shock that he was the only one stark naked.

Quickly he jerked around, turning his back to the others, and washed off his soap and shampoo. Then, grabbing his clothes from the shelf, he shot out of the bathroom, only to run into two dressed women who were coming down the steps from the floor above. They arrived just in time to get a rear view of the bare new teacher as he dashed for his room.

Nothing further happened, but he had learned that Thais do not normally bathe naked in communal facilities. They use a *sarong*-type tube of cloth to hide in, wriggle around to soap everywhere, and then stand to splash it off. Still wet, the sarong wearer will slip into a dry cloth before leaving to get dressed. It's very modest, and the Thais are modest. More modern Thais still will shower in public places in their underwear, then put on dry underwear afterwards, underneath a towel or *sarong*.

During the Japanese occupation, Japanese soldiers would march naked, brush and soap in hand, from their barracks to the nearest *khlong* for their bath, and march back equally bare. The Thais have never forgotten this and call naked bathing a 'Japanese bath.'

175

The times, and what's fashionable, are changing everywhere. For Thais to pay respects to Her Majesty the Princess Mother in 1996, they were told in the public media what to wear and what would not be allowed. In the old days, everybody would have known already, except for *farangs*, perhaps. Western suits and ties, as foreign and uncomfortable as they may be, are now considered *de rigueur* in some circles.

The driver of a *tuk-tuk* was once elected to parliament. For the opening session, he drove his *tuk-tuk* up the drive to Parliament House and just as quickly back down the drive again—the guards would not allow him to enter in his low-status vehicle. Another man, a farmer, tried to ride his water buffalo to parliament but was turned back, too. These vehicles, however honest their owners' professions, were not considered *moh som*.

Phak-Phuak

Pronounced 'puk-pooak' and meaning your 'gang,' your 'buddies,' your 'peer group.' There is no escaping *phak-phuak* and its ramifications in Thai business, politics, the military, and even between individuals or families. This is the network of friendships, often made in school or the military academy, that can affect everyone. Often, it is between the students of a

particular class or year. It is about the only relationship in Thailand that might supersede family relationships for the demand on a Thai's loyalty. The expat is often mildly surprised to learn that the university rector and a dean or department head may be cousins. It comes as a deeper revelation to find that the janitor may be a cousin, too! *Phak-phuak* comes into play often in a Thai's life, and an expat is at a great disadvantage if he or she does not develop one or join one. The absence of a *phak-phuak* leaves one isolated, unsupported, and alone. This is a situation that is unimaginably horrible to the average Thai. And woe to the unaware expat who makes a Thai enemy. He hasn't made just one. Everyone in that person's *phak-phuak* are now his enemies, as well. It can work both ways.

The Five S's

Here are some further qualities that a Thai usually thinks important. They are sometimes taught in Thai schools as the 'Five S's.'

Sa-at

'Clean' or in order. This means 'clean' in a moral sense as well as simply the physical absence of dirt.

Suphap

'Polite,' sometimes in odd ways. A bus driver can be *suphap* if he stops long enough to allow passengers to disembark safely and doesn't cut off other vehicles. Wearing trousers instead of a *phakhaoma* or a *sarong* may be *suphap* when entertaining guests at home. Too-tight slacks for girls, or too short shorts, are usually *mai suphap* ('not polite'). For Muslims, Burmese, and Malays, *sarongs* for men are *suphap* as they are part of the national or religious dress. How one speaks or behaves is either polite or not polite. Many things are *suphap* or *mai suphap* across cultures, so this one may be a bit easier to learn than some of the others.

Samruam

This means 'decorous,' 'restrained,' and 'proper' behaviour. You can see its connection with *chai yen* and *chai rawn*, mentioned previously.

Sometimes it's okay to give this one up, though. An example might be the traditional Thai New Year's celebration in mid-April, called Songkran. Officially and in common practice, everybody starts off with a quality of proper comportment, known as *samruam*, or the sprinkling of a few drops of perfume on the Buddha images, then on the monks and grandparents and parents. But very shortly the affair gets raucous and boisterous, and is not at all *samruam*, as water by the bucketful and even from fire hoses is tossed everywhere.

A monk, out on his alms-receiving round for food, should walk decorously, his eyes on the ground ahead of him. If he sashays about, his eyes glancing to the left and right, then he is not *samruam*, and he will be criticized for this.

Sanuk

It's extremely important that an activity, film, game, play, book—anything, really—be 'fun,' or *sanuk*. Frequently, Thais consider *sanuk* the things the *farang* expat may not react to very well. To laugh (inappropriately, according to *farang*) during the sad scenes in a movie is tantamount to behaving badly. But the Thais can find this *sanuk* quality in many very ordinary situations.

A word in Thai that helps the jollity of the Thais is *ngaan*. *Ngaan* means 'work,' but it also means 'pleasure.' Illustrative of this are several terms all using *ngaan*. Study these and you'll see how central pleasure and having fun are in Thai life and values: *ngaan liang* ('party,' or dinner party); *taeng ngaan* ('wedding,' 'to marry'); *ngaan khuen pi mai* ('New Year party'); *ngaan chalong* ('festival,' 'celebration'); *ngaan chalerm* ('royal celebration,' 'celebration of a royal birthday'); *ngaan lilaat* ('dancing party,' 'dance'); *ngaan wat* ('temple fair').

Ngaan then is the kind of word that shines a light on Thai attitudes toward work, function, and pleasurable occupation.

Saduak

This literally means 'convenient,' though perhaps not always as expats might judge things. When I first came to Thailand, roads and bridges were being built all across the kingdom. One result was that the boat services were slowly being discarded in favour of buses. When I asked where the nearest boat pier was, I'd often get the response, "*Pai rot di kwa*," or "Go by vehicle is better." By that they meant 'more *saduak*,' more convenient. It's easy for me to let a bus pass me by so long as I have an alternative. The boat services were more fun, more interesting, and less crowded. Also, the boats were not equipped with ghetto blasters to render

me simple with their noise. Boat engines were loud enough, thank you, and while all the Thais were going by bus, I hung out for boats wherever I could. That may be hopelessly old-fashioned, but then as a *farang*, I'm considered weird by Thais anyhow. "*Pai ruea di kwa!*" is what I taunt now. "Go by boat is better!"

This *saduak* business in its negative, *mai saduak*, 'not convenient,' covers lots of territory and often gives an excuse for not doing things that don't have to be expanded upon. Something, like cleaning the refrigerator this morning, might well be avoided by declaring the task to be *mai saduak* right now. Maybe later . . . perhaps. Remember, too, that if it has rained, is raining, or looks like it might rain, you can use *mai saduak*—the inconvenience of trying to get around—as an acceptable pretext for not doing whatever it is you're avoiding. Come to think of it, you can use it as an acceptable excuse even if the skies are clear blue. It would be *mai suphap* to ask any further question if you say that something or other was *mai saduak*.

What About. . . ? Time, Titles, Toilets, and Other Tidbits

Food, Wonderful Food

It would be a remiss author indeed who could write a book about Thailand and barely mention this country's cuisine, particularly as Thai food is conquering the culinary world. There is hardly a town or city accessible to travellers or tourists that doesn't boast at least one 'Thai restaurant.' If there isn't one, then it must be an off-the-path place indeed.

I use the inverted commas around 'Thai restaurant' because some of them, while passing for Thai, are really owned and run by Chinese. It doesn't make a lot of difference, as most of the restaurants in Bangkok are owned and operated by Chinese or their children. The menu is at least mixed. Except in Isaan, it would be hard to find a pure Thai foodshop.

In Isaan and Northern Thailand there are some differences, usually based on their preference for *khao niao*, the glutinous 'sticky rice' that

you eat with your fingers. In Bangkok, outside of the Isaan restaurants and foodshops, *khao niao* is generally known as the base for sweets—such as with condensed milk and fresh, ripe mango; or served with *som tam*, ('spicy papaya salad').

There are many fine cookbooks for Thai cuisine—or mixed Thai-Chinese—one by a former teacher where I worked, who wrote a recipe book for making Thai food in non-Thai kitchens. This was aimed at those expats who went back home hungry for Thai tastes. The author had to suggest many substitutes for herbs used here that were unknown or unavailable in the West. This situation has eased a lot with heavy Asian migration elsewhere. Nowadays, in any town or city with a large Asian population—be they Filipinos, Vietnamese, Khmers, Lao, Hmongs, or Thais—it is not hard to find a market where at least one vendor specializes in purveying *phrik khi nu* ('mouse-shit peppers'), which enliven Asian cuisines (and burn the tongues out of some unaware *farangs*), or what Thais call *nam pla*, the salty fish sauce that they seem to use on just about anything.

Here are some standard dishes for you to go out and try. All are Thai, but some are also Chinese:

Nuea phat nam man hoi—beef sliced and fried in oyster sauce;

Kai phat met mamuang himaphan—chicken fried with cashew nuts, onions, and large chillies;

Phanaeng nuea—beef curry;

Phat prio wan mu (kai, kung, pla muek)—fried sweet
and sour pork (or chicken, shrimp, or squid);

Pla muek thod krathiem phrik thai—squid fried with
garlic and black pepper;

Tom kha kai—ginger soup with chicken and coconut milk;

Khai yat sai—stuffed omelette;

Khai jio mu sap—omelette with chopped pork;

Khai kata—egg, pork sausage, shredded pork;

Pla sam rot—sea fish in a sour-sweet-and-salty sauce;

Tom yam kung—the spicy national soup, with
shrimp and lemon grass;

Yam pla duk fu—fluffed up mudfish (despite the name,
it's delicious);

Kai (nuea, mu) phat kraphao—fried hot and spicy chicken
(or beef or pork) with basil leaf;

Nuea phat phrik—beef fried with green chillies;

Nuea san—actually a Western dish of beef fillet;

Pu phat phong kari—fried crab with curry powder.

Popular drinks include:

Nam yen—cold water;

Nam soda—cold soda water;

Nam som khan—freshly squeezed orange juice, often with salt in it (*Mai sai kluea*, 'Don't put salt in it');

Nam manao—lemon drink, lemonade;

Oliang—iced sweet black coffee;

Cha yen—iced tea with milk;

Cha dam yen—iced tea without milk;

Kafae rawn—hot coffee, usually with evaporated milk;

Kafae yen—iced coffee with milk;

Bia—beer, of which there are many brands (most common are *bia* Singha [pronounced 'sing'], *bia* Kloster, or *bia* Heineken);

Nam khaeng plao mai sai nam—a glass of ice without water.

Squat Toilets:
A Slip-Up Could Be a Nasty Experience

However you fancify it with a porcelain foundation, a squat toilet is still basically a hole in the floor. Because these type of amenities are more common in continental Europe and parts of Latin America, they don't appear to scare nationals of those countries. Like the *bidet* that confronts many Americans with a dilemma (For washing feet? Socks? A fountain for playing with while attending to serious business?), the squat toilet is

a thing of terror for some. Unlike the *bidet*, everyone understands what the squat toilet is for, but using it is something else again.

The squat toilet has its supporters, though. They claim the user will lessen the risk of haemorrhoids, will enjoy a faster and more complete evacuation, and the thing itself is cheaper to install and easier to keep clean. (Do I hear a complaint that if they are so much easier to keep clean, why, in much of the world, including Thailand, are these facilities so often smelly, filthy, unpleasant places?)

Opponents of squat toilets will tell tales of users falling over on their backs or (horror!) unintentionally relieving themselves onto the backs of their shoes or into their trouser cuffs. Or of losing their loose change, car keys, and wallets down the hole.

Most modern public buildings, big hotels, and progressive business firms will provide sit-toilets in their restrooms, but may devote one stall to the traditional squat kind. Many shopping malls do just the reverse: a line of stalls with squat toilets and one sit-down type on the end.

There is also the matter of cleaning oneself. The tradition in most of Asia is to wash with the left hand. This explains why gifts are never offered with that hand. In such public facilities, a water trough and plastic scoop are usually provided for the purpose. Toilet paper might possibly be found in most sit-down cubicles, or, more often than not, there will be an empty roller device where it *should* be found. Most people have learned to carry toilet paper or tissues for the many times it is not available. There may also extend from the wall a short hosepipe with its own nozzle to accommodate those who wash.

Small-diameter drainpipes and tightly compressed wads of toilet paper make a bad combination, as those who have spent hours extracting everything from wads of tissue, soiled underwear, hankies, and strips of newspaper well know. There are also those users who attempt to flush sanitary napkins down the hole, as well. This may require a professional plumber to fix.

How to Use a Squat Toilet.

For everybody who wants to know but has been too shy to ask, here's a brief statement of how to use a squat toilet:

Aside from issues of cleanlisness, a number of questions will already be facing the potential user of the squat toilet—Thais included. It can be a daunting prospect. A black and stinking concrete pedestal with a hole

in it? A flooded floor? A toilet-paper roller with actual toilet paper? (If not, get out your packet of tissues.) A hosepipe and water tap that work? Is there a hook on the door for bags and jackets and the like? Is there a bucket or wastebasket for bits of trash and wadded, used toilet paper? (Most Thai toilets will provide this to discourage tossing it in the drain.) Is there a filled tank for washing the bowl and another for washing you? And a scoop for dipping the water? If everything appears in order and there is no lurking lizard or hairy creature to pounce on you, you're all set:

Squat down on your haunches, pulling up your skirt or your pant cuffs, placing your feet on the shoe-shaped platforms on either side of the hole, and be very careful not to slip off. It is my experience that few *farangs* can achieve this contortion with much grace. Thais, Japanese, and some other Asians have shorter lower-leg bones—(tibiae and fibulae) between the ankle and the knee—than most Westerners, and therefore find squatting more comfortable. Better balanced and with a lower centre of gravity than the average *farang*, Asians seldom topple over onto their sides and backs.

You may find it easier to straddle the whole toilet rather than to stand on the platform. Many who are unused to the squat toilets also may not have a very good aim so as to hit the bowl dead centre. Practice makes perfect!

I have also found that many *farangs* have a problem in maintaining their precarious perch while wiping or using one hand to grab the water dipper, fill it, carry it into position, and then, with the other hand, tend to their bottoms. Of course, this seems to require three hands. You also have to have a firm grip on your clothes! Possibly a fourth hand will seem necessary if you're balancing against the wall. (Not the door, please. It may fly open and—well, there you sprawl.) This whole symphony of movements requires some practice, but you can learn it all more quickly than it took to describe. Soon you'll have it choreographed correctly so that you can emerge relieved, clean, and dry.

Clothing has a lot to do with convenient use of a squat toilet. Men who wear a *sarong* and women in loose skirts will have an easier time of it than those with tight-fitting jeans, skirts, or slacks. One tip: once you're inside the cubicle and the door is shut, take off the nether garments and hook them on a nail, handle, or hook, if available. Thus disencumbered, you may find the whole experience more manageable.

By the way, should there be two tanks or troughs for water storage in the toilet, the smaller or lower one is the water for flushing into and around the toilet bowl. The taller, larger one is for bathing, not to soak your soiled clothes in or to soak yourself in on a hot day. It is, by the bye, very polite of you to refill a nearly emptied tank from the nearby tap.

Don't let the whole idea scare you too much. Treat it as another experience in the exotic East. And good luck!

Yoo-Hoo! Where Are You?
Addresses, Postal Services, Communications, Customs, and Titles

Addresses

In Thornton Welder's play, *Our Town*, one of the characters tells another about a letter, and mentions the address? All of it is there: name of the recipient, Grover's Corner, Sutton County, New Hampshire, the United States of America, Western Hemisphere, Earth, the Solar System, the Universe, and then the "Mind of God." Addresses written Thai style are a bit like that, smallest unit first, then the next and the next largest, and so on, but not all the way to the "Mind of God." A typical Thai mailing address follows a similar pattern:

> Khun Prasert Ramvong,
> House 12/3, Village 4,
> So-and-so subdistrict,
> So-and-so district,
> So-and-so province, 20020.

Thailand is divided into 76 provinces (*changwat*). Provinces are divided into districts (*amphur*). Each district has several sub-districts (*tambon*, or *tambol*). This is still the basic pattern for Thai addresses, especially upcountry, which is defined as anywhere outside Bangkok. Nowadays, a five-digit postal code (*rahat praisani*) will be added to the name of the province.

City addresses are sometimes shorter:

Khun Prasert Pamvong,
12/2 Sukhumvit Soi 33,
Bangkok, 10110.

In this form, 12 is the street address that corresponds to a block or plot. Often the block or plot numbers are not sequential. The house is number 2, which may be in a compound or is part of a subdivided plot, on lane number 33 off Sukhumvit Road, in the 10110 postal code.

Postal Services and Communications

The Thai postal service allows the sending of express and registered letters both within Thailand and abroad. EMS—Express Mail Service—is both expensive and fast, the same as elsewhere. There are also private firms that handle courier services, and these may be even more expensive. Still, if time and reliability are of the essence, these services may prove just what you need.

Registered mail with 'Return Reply Requested' costs a few baht more than ordinary mail, but you will then receive a slip indicating the letter has been received at the other end, showing date, time, and by whom. As the additional tariff is only a few baht, many expats are used to routinely registering their letters for Thailand delivery. For overseas, this service is only available for certain countries and can raise the postage costs considerably. Still, if you're paying bills by cheque, it is nice to know if it arrived at the destination.

Most Thai telephone services, other than cellular, are divided between the TOT Corporation Public Company Limited (TOT) for domestic service, and the Communications Authority of Thailand (CAT) for long-distance service. Your telephone bills will come from one or the other, depending upon which call you have made. It seems to depend upon which kind of phone exchange to which you're connected. For many years it was difficult to get phones and even harder to get a listing in the telephone directories. Now you can probably get a telephone within days or up to a few weeks (depending upon where you live). You also may order your lines from one of the private suppliers, such as TRUE (formerly TelecomAsia) or TT & T. Directory listings are still not easy, and usually show the name of the owner of the phone, such as a landlord, and not the user or current residence occupant. Mobile phones are easily available at competitive prices from three main service providers using GSM digital networks: Digital Total Access Communications (DTAC), TA Orange, and Advanced Info Services (AIS).

E-mail service is widely available through about a dozen private companies, such as CSLoxinfo or KSC, for personal and corporate accounts. Pre-paid or subscription services are available. Pre-paid software is available in bookshops or computer program outlets, enabling you to hook up and use the service for a month or more. For regular, full-time service, the packaging will give you contact details.

Customs

There are fairly strict Customs rules in Thailand, particularly for things sent in by post. If there is a package of goods subject to a duty, you will get a notice from the post office to pick it up (perhaps at Customs or maybe at the post office), and there you'll have to pay the duty. For example, books are duty free; underwear and sweaters are not. Unless you have access to an embassy's special pouch or the APO (Army Post Office, which the American Embassy uses for its officials), I would recommend you tell your correspondents not to send in dutiable goods. There are also very strict censorship rules. So don't try to have things like *Playboy* sent here. They may be subject to seizure, or will simply get 'lost' in the mail.

Abbreviations for Titles

There are several titles you might find abbreviated in newspapers, name cards, invitations, and other places. Aside from the more obvious ones such Dr., or HM for His or Her Majesty, these include:

TM—Their Majesties;

HRM—His/Her Royal Highness;

HSH—His/Her Serene Highness;

HH—His/Her Highness;

MC—*Mom Chao*, a grandchild of a king;

MR—*Mom Rajawong*, a child of an MC;

ML—*Mom Luang*, a child of an MR;

HE—His Excellency;

Ven.—Venerable, for monks.

Khunying and *Thanpuying* are women's titles, something like the British 'Dame' or 'Lady,' and are always used with the first name, or first and last names together, but never the last name alone.

There are also a lot of military and academic titles, similar to those used abroad, and often copied from them.

You should remember that Thais almost always use their first names. Their last names are appropriately and politely reserved for official use, except upon introduction. After the introduction has been made, the last name can be omitted.

Thai Time

Only a manual labourer, a boatman, or a farmer will not display a wrist-watch while working. Watches, among many other items, are status symbols amongst Thais. But that doesn't necessarily mean they use them to tell the time.

Let's say you're walking along the street with a Thai friend, Khun Somsak, and you run into a mutual acquaintance, Khun Lamduan. After the *sawatdi*s and the inevitable "*Pai nai?*" ('Where are you going?'), to which Lamduan answers, "*Plao*" ('nowhere' or 'nothing'), Somsak says, "*Pai du nang kan mai?*" ('Let's go to a movie together.')

As Lamduan nods his acquiescence, Somsak adds, "*Phob kan na Lido,*" which you understand as 'See you at the Lido cinema.'

Lamduan then asks, "*Ki mong?*" ('At what time?' Literally, 'How many hours?')

Then Somsak says something that you find incomprehensible. He says, "*Song thum.*" ('Two drumstrokes.')

Lamduan understands and goes on his way with a nod and smile to you, after replying, "Two drumstrokes, then. See you."

Somsak turns to you with a smile and explains, "He'll meet us at the Lido at two."

"Two?"

"Yeah, at two tonight. We'll see the movie then."

You're an expat, you understand a bit of Thai, but you have no intention of being anywhere but at home in bed at 2:00 a.m. tonight. What's going on here?

What has happened, of course, is that you've run head on into the Thai expressions for time, which are very different from those in the international circles you may have been moving in.

And in any event, if it rains, Somsak and Lamduan will probably not meet you at all, anywhere.

Rainwater dissolves all appointments.

You may never have noticed back home this quality of rainwater, but in Thailand nobody will take it amiss if you skip your appointment because it is raining. Rain is a fine, popular, and much accepted excuse for missing any kind of appointment. Rain makes the traffic worse (at least

in Bangkok and Chiang Mai), and traffic jams may make it impossible to make the date even if you really wanted to.

Without rain, Lamduan and Somsak will meet at the Lido at 8:00 p.m. and wonder where you are. They may wait outside, too, under the marquee till the film has started. By then they'll have decided you've found something else to do, and so they go in.

The Thai system of telling time is an old one, far older than our midnight to 12:00 noon and over to midnight again. Certainly both of these systems are older than the 24-hour scheme employed by schedule makers and the Western military. The Thai system was used long before clocks and watches reached the kingdom, and is still widely used by Thais just about anywhere in the country. Here is the way it works:

The day is divided into groups of hours that are based on the light, or lack of it, and on how the time was announced in the days before watches. While we may have trouble with this system, give a thought to the Thai who finds our system confusing, or the newer 24-hour arrangement, which is not represented on the faces of most clocks and watches at all.

First, here are some important terms: *ti* (*dtee*) refers to strokes, in this case usually on a piece of metal. *Ti* literally means 'to beat' something or someone. *Mong* (*moang*) means 'hour.' *Chao* (*chow*) refers to 'morning,' *bai* (*bye*) to 'afternoon.' *Yen* means 'cool,' as in the late-afternoon cool of the day. So *yen* logically is also used to mean 'early evening.' *Thum* (*toom*) is the sound a drum makes. Drums are still used in temples to summon the monks to eat. The two expressions *thiang khuen* and *thiang wan* refer to 'night-time' (*khuen*) and 'daytime' (*wan*), respectively, and take the place of our midnight and noon. In Thai, the word 'hours' as used in the 24-hour clock will be replaced by the word *nalika* (*nah-lee-gah*), which refers to hours of time in counting.

Western Standard	Traditional Thai
Midnight	*Thiang khuen*
1:00 a.m.	*Ti nueng* (*dtee* 1)
2:00 a.m.	*Ti song* (*dtee* 2)
3:00 a.m.	*Ti sam* (*dtee* 3)
4:00 a.m.	*Ti si* (*dtee* 4)
5:00 a.m.	*Ti ha* (*dtee* 5)
6:00 a.m.	*Hok* (6) *mong chao*
7:00 a.m.	*Nueng* (1) *mong chao*
8:00 a.m.	*Song* (2) *mong chao*
9:00 a.m.	*Sam* (3) *mong chao*
10:00 a.m.	*Si* (4) *mong chao*
11:00 a.m.	*Ha* (5) *mong chao*
12:00 noon	*Thiang wan*
1:00 p.m.	*Bai mong*
2:00 p.m.	*Bai song mong*
3:00 p.m.	*Bai sam mong*
4:00 p.m.	*Bai si mong*, or *si mong yen*
5:00 p.m.	*Ha mong yen*
6:00 p.m.	*Hok mong yen*
7:00	*Nueng thum*
8:00	*Song thum*
9:00	*Sam thum*
10:00	*Si thum*
11:00	*Ha thum*

Are you ready to flush your watch down the toilet? Are you rushing out to buy a sundial? Many Thais are still close enough to nature to be able to look up at the sky and determine the approximate time. Can you?

Another feature of Thai time is that anywhere from 9:00 a.m. to 9:59 a.m. is all 9:00 a.m.—or *sam* (3) *mong chao*, old style. One is not culpably late till 10:00 a.m.—*si* (4) *mong chao*. If you're late, no Thai will get upset, nor to be sure will Spaniards, Brazilians, Arabs, and many other nationalities. But what about Americans? Some studies have shown that after about five minutes the Anglo-American is getting uptight. After 15 minutes, he's ready to blow.

For a farming country where people travelled a lot by boat or buffalo carts and only had to judge the rise and fall of the tides, the Thai systems were fine. It's only since the introduction of more modern and exact systems of scheduling that the need came about for something a bit more finely tuned, even to nanoseconds in some industries.

It's an unusual Thai who'd be motivated by mere clock time. It's the rare American who can rest content without seconds, minutes, and hours. The difference can cause confusion, irritation, or even more severe problems unless all parties involved in setting dates and times are aware of these differences between Thai and Western frames of reference.

Hey, You! and Other Names

Besides their surname, Thais generally have two names: their nicknames, given at birth, and their proper name—as will be used on official documents. Let's look at the very first name they're given: their nicknames:

A nickname is given at birth and usually sticks to a person throughout their lives. Surprisingly, these names are not always elevating. These might include Ma ('Dog'), Mu ('Pig'), Mi ('Bear'), Ma ('Horse'), Daeng ('Red'), Nu ('Rat'), and Pho ('Enough'). One can only wonder if Enough's mother felt that way at the prospect of having yet another child.

Some names are nonsense syllables like Ningnong or O. Others are off-putting, yet descriptive, such as Kung ('Shrimp,' for a small baby), Phak ('Vegetable'), Samphao ('Sailing Vessel') and Ott ('Pollywog' or 'Tadpole'). Att, Eet, It, Uht, and Oot mean little or nothing, but are easy to say and easily remembered. Miss Universe of a few years ago was named Pui, which sounds nice and literally means 'the tight sleep of a baby,' but another meaning is 'fertilizer.'

Why These Strange Nicknames?

This naming tradition goes back to ancient and primitive beliefs that a child bearing a lovely, proper, or official name would be at risk from the envy of an unhappy demon. Best give the baby a nickname that won't attract unwelcome attention.

If a child of Buddhist parents survives its first thirty days, it is time to ask a monk for its real, official name. When a man is born, he gets a nickname (Uan, or 'Fatty,' for example), then he will be given an official name based on the letters of the alphabet that correspond to the time of his birth. If he was born on Thursday (*Wan Pharuehatsabodi*), his new name will come from a line of consonants in the alphabet: p, ph, b, bh, and m. The monk will look in a names book, rather like those that Western parents sometimes employ. He will select a name that starts with the right consonant, sounds good, and has an auspicious meaning.

Many women acquire names beginning with the syllable *Su*, which means 'beautiful' or 'excellent': Sumali, Supani, Sunari, and so on. Each has a meaning, very often poetic or literary, which is beautified with the prefix *su* to mean a 'Bouquet of Beautiful Blossoms,' 'Beautiful Hands,' 'Beautiful Girl.' *Su* is less common for men's names but there are some. Sunai, Suchai, Sucharit—'Beautiful Eyes,' 'Handsome Male,' 'Honest.'

Many names reflect memory of war: Thongchai ('Flag of Victory'), or Chainarong ('Victorious Campaign')—or desired qualities, such as Prasert ('Excellent'), Pradit ('Inventive') or Bancha ('Command'), and so on.

Girls' names reflect more feminine qualities: Somrak ('Proper Love'), or the names of flowers: Kulaap ('Rose'). Or there is Saengchan ('Moonlight'), Nimnuan ('Soft and Delicate'), Noknoi ('Little Bird'), and so on.

Until 1917, surnames were not found necessary, but King Rama VI imposed them on his subjects as part of his efforts to modernize the country. People of high class were often awarded long, high-sounding, polysyllabic names from Sanskrit or Pali. Commoners got shorter or even monosyllabic last names, usually Thai in origin. The variety of names is impressive and some holders are fiercely proud of theirs because they were awarded by the king rather than by a mere clerk in a district office.

Occasionally you will meet someone whose last name includes *na* (not capitalized). An example of this would be Khun Krisda Arunwongse na Ayudhya (a former governor of Bangkok). Arunwongse is his last name; na Ayudhya is the particle indicating that one of his ancestors was royalty. All of these *na* names are followed by place names. Na Chiang Mai or na Songkhla are examples.

Because they traditionally went without surnames, Thais now generally use their titles with their first names, their surnames only being used to complete an identification:

Interior Minister Sanan (Khajornprasat);

General Chainarong (Nunphakdi);

Doctor Kitti (Angsusingh);

Achaan (or 'Professor') Krirkkiat (Adun).

Nai, *Nang*, *Nangsao*, or Mr., Mrs., and Miss are commonly used, as well. Ms. is rarely recognized in Thailand.

Phra ('Venerable') Kamala Bhikkhu is another example of a name and title. In this case, *phra* and *bhikkhu* both mean 'monk.' *Phra* adorns

any name to make it sacred or to elevate it further, as well as to recognize respect for it.

A married woman uses her first name. Many professional women, as in the West, keep their own family names, or use both family and married names. Achaan Mattani Mojdara Ruttnin is a well-known university teacher, writer, and theatre director. *Achaan* means 'teacher,' Mattani is her official first name, Mojdara is her maiden name, Ruttnin is her husband's family name. We didn't inquire about her unofficial nickname.

Note that there is no way in Thai of saying on invitations or introductions 'Mr. and Mrs. John Smith.' As both names use *Khun* for Mr., Mrs., and Miss, it would probably take this form: Khun Banyat Banthadthan and wife; Doctor Krasae and Professor Sunari Phattanakanchanakul would also be an appropriate form of addressing a couple.

For children of school age, the title will be *dekchai* ('boy child') or *dekying* ('girl child'). A nickname may well be used with the title *dek*: Dekying Sinidh Chandrakunphong might also be known less officially as Dekying Noi.

Chinese Immigrants in Thailand

A special variation of names is used by Chinese immigrants to Thailand. They use amongst their Chinese friends the traditional Chinese arrangement of clan plus personal name or names: Li Hung-chang; Chiang Kai-shek; Mao Ze-dong (though sometimes the hyphen is dropped), Mao Zedong (or Tse-tung)

Often Thais will write these names with the term *sae* ('clan'), inverting the order to accord more with Thai practice: Hungchang (or Hung Chang) sae Li (or Lee); Kai-shek sae Chiang.

But when any immigrant tries for naturalization, he must 'Siamese' his name. It is required by law that Thai subjects must have Thai names. Li (Lee) may thus try to preserve part of his old name: Krungkrai Liphattanakanchanadhurakijkul

His old Chinese friends who knew him as Li will still call him that, but the Interior Ministry further orders that anyone adopting a Thai surname may not use one that others are already using. Our friend Li here has simply added to his surname till it is very unlikely anyone will have the same combination and thus the same name. To do so, he may have simply added some high-sounding words that relate to his business:

Phattana—'to develop'; Kanchana—'gold'; Dhurakij—'business'; Kun (or Kul)—'family' or 'clan.'

Everyone knows he's Chinese either because of the remaining Chinese last name, Li (or Lee), or because of its length and meaning. But this is not necessarily the end of old Li's problems. If he should, by any fluke, be named in the *Bangkok Post* or *The Nation*, his name will have to be run through the process of Romanization for the English reader.

Changing Thai, written in Thai letters, to Thai written in Roman ABCs is tricky, as we have seen, and the official system is often ignored by the press. What we have seen—Liphattanakanchanadhurakijkul—could come out as Leepatanakarnchanatoorakitkool, or some other variation.

Anyone learning the type of Romanization approved by the Royal Institute (called the *Rajabandhitayasathaan* system) will probably fling himself from the nearest high window. Please don't. Few Thais are familiar with this system at all, and as so many have studied a course or two of English somewhere along the line, they may well try to write it in English, as in the previous example.

Other groups in the kingdom, permanent or passing through, have their own ways of handling names in their own languages. As Thais of whatever background, they will somewhere in their documents and booklets have their new Thai-style name set out in Thai letters while retaining, in some form, their own ethnic identities.

Monks, too, present a naming problem. As a newly-ordained monk, the Thai will use whatever name he was awarded from the name book, but as he goes up in monastic rank, he will change his name to something more impressive. It sounds more complicated than it is, but this also used to happen with commoners who attained the lower ranks of the nobility. Rising higher, his name was changed again and again to reflect his increasing status. This is sometimes shown in writing with his original name in parentheses, so everyone will know who he was and is.

One example of this is the abbot of the temple where I was ordained, who went through these transformations:

Daeng—his nickname given at birth (it means 'red'); Kamon—the name given Daeng by a monk one month after his birth; Phra Kamala—his ordination name (in this case Kamon and Kamala are written the same in Thai. Both mean 'lotus'); Phra Mahâ Kamon—when he received an advanced degree in Pali studies, he reverted to the use of his own name preceded by the title *mahâ*, equivalent to a university doctorate.

When he received the further rank of *phra khru* ('religious teacher'), his name changed yet again to the sonorous Phra Khru Samvarasama-dhivatra, pronounced Sangvornsamathiwat. Had he lived longer, perhaps he would have attained the highest princely rank as the *samdej phra sangharaja*, the 'patriarch' or 'king of the monks.' That would have brought an even more august moniker and would have warranted the use of the special *rajasap* ('royal language'), based on Sanskrit and Khmer and similar to that used for the king and queen and others in the royal family. Even many Thais do not use it well, though they may understand a bit when listening to the news on radio and television. Some years ago, one of the princesses had an appendectomy and it took me three weeks of asking to find out why she was in the hospital.

Sometimes expats find they have been given a Thai name by co-workers or friends. This is usually informal and can be a demonstration of affection and acceptance. Sometimes it is critical and based on spite, but then the expat may never hear of it. I was given a name based on a misunderstanding of my name arrangement when I became a monk.

The name given me at my ordination was Mahâviro, partly because it was a name in the 'name book' that would be pronounced more or less the same by Thais or *farang*. It was also the name of the founder of the Jain religion, one strikingly similar to Buddhism. This proved confusing to both monks and laypeople. The *mahâ* caused eyebrows to rise and *wais* to grow more profound as many people took it as an educational rank, like Ph.D.

"Imagine!" I overheard a woman say. "Three days in the monkhood and he's a *mahâ* already!"

Before I was ordained, I was Roger, or Yod (George), as explained earlier. After my ordination, I became Viro, or Viroj, to those who had met me while I was in robes. Another name that stuck to me was a recognition that I was gaining weight and ageing. Only by accident did I learn my manager was calling me Lung Uan, 'Fat Uncle,' or 'Uncle Fatso.' It may have been accurate enough, but I was sensitive enough to find it annoying.

Most Thais, when they know it, call me by my professional rank: *achaan*. I was a lecturer for several years at two universities in Bangkok, so I was Achaan Roger in the Thai manner, or Achaan Welty in a hybrid

Thai-*farang* way. In either case people have trouble saying my names. Roger often comes out like an attempt to say 'royal' but with an 'n' sound rather than an 'l' at the end. As for my surname, it is often deformed to *Wen-tee* with the accent at the end, *Wen-TEE*!

Today, people who don't know my background will call me Khun ('Mr.') Roger or Khun Welty. That's all right. Chinese shopkeepers have a way of labelling customers as *Nai* ('Mr.') or *nai hang* (which is like 'boss'). A Thai who'd studied British English might well call me Master.

The form of address heard for a long time here was based on the former presence of American military personnel: 'Hey, you!' The best response to that was not to give the offenders a stern lecture on proper manners, which would be difficult to get across the language barrier at any rate. It's best just to wave back and smile.

Smiles go a long way in Thailand, as I keep emphasizing.

Selected Glossary

achaan teacher
ahimsa harmlessness toward all beings
amphur district
avuso friend

bai afternoon
bai samkhan thin thi residence permit
bat prachachon citizen's identity card
bhâvanâ spiritual and mental development
bhikkhu Buddhist monk
bhikkhuni Buddhist 'nuns'
bia beer

chai rawn hot-hearted/hot-headed
chai yen cool-hearted/being patient
changwat province
chao morning
chao arwat abbot of a monastery (*wat*)
chao thai phu khao hilltribes ('Thai people from the hills')
chedi Buddhist stupa
chek immigrant Chinese (derog.)
chongkraben traditional lower garment (gathered, drawn, and tucked)

dâna generosity
dek child
deva angelic being
deva-raja god-king
Dhamma the Buddha's 'Teaching'
dukkha in Buddhism, everything that is unsatisfactory

farang white foreigner
feng shui geomancy

hai kiat giving honour, dignity, and respect to ones elders or superiors

kaan buat Buddhist ordination
karunâ compassion
khaek guest/Indians, Arabs, Muslims, Hindus, Sikhs (derog.)
khao rice
khao niao glutinous sticky rice
khlong canal
khon cheen Chinese people
khon khaek 'guest people' (see *khaek*)
khon masked drama
khon tangchat person of another race, life, or birth/foreigners
khon Thai Thai people
khop khun maak thank you very much
khuen night-time
khun you
khunying female honorific title (like the British 'dame' or 'lady')
khwai water buffalo
kong tek Chinese funeral
kreng chai considerate/unassuming

lakhon play/drama
likay musical folk drama
luk khreung of mixed race
luuk thung Thai country music

maak chewed concoction of betel leaves, areca nuts, and lime paste
mae chi devout Buddhist laywoman/'nun'
mae sue female matchmaker/wedding organizer
mahâ great (prefix)
mahâraja great king
mai pen rai never mind/it doesn't matter/it's okay
mettâ loving kindness
mia chao hired wife

mia noi minor wife
moh doctor
moh-lam bawdy northeastern folk music
moho angry
moh som appropriate/suitable/fitting
mong hour
muang Thai Thailand
mudîtâ sympathetic joy
muu baan village

nai inside
nai master/boss
nakieng gangster
nalika clock
nam chai generosity
nang yai/nang talung shadow-puppet theatre
ngaan work
ngaan chalong festival/celebration
ngaan sob funeral
ngaan wat temple fair
ngiu Chinese opera
nibbana nirvana
nimon invitation
nok outside
nong younger

pai go
pai nai? where are you going?
phak-phuak gang of friends/peer group
phakhaoma traditional wrap-around sarong
pha sin traditional, long formal skirt
phi ghost
phi older/elder
phinphaat/piphat traditional Thai orchestra/Thai classical music
phra honorific for gods, noblemen, Buddha images, palaces, temples,
    monks, or anything special, sanctified, or holy
phra chao lord/king

phra khru religious or spiritual teacher
pindabat alms collecting
praisani post office
prathom school grade/school year

rahat praisani postal code
rajasap royal language/dialect

saduak convenient
sai sin a Brahmanical cord
saksri concept concerning dignity, self-image, and self-esteem.
sala pavillion/hall
samlor trishaw
samruam decorous/restrained/proper behaviour
Sangha the order of Buddhist monks
san phra bhumi/san prah poom spirit house
sanuk fun
saphan bridge
sasana religion
sawatdi hello/goodbye
sîla morality
soi lane/street
suphap polite

taeng ngaan wedding/to marry
talaat market
tambon sub-district
tha dock/pier/jetty
thabian baan household registration
thanpuying female honorific title (like the British 'dame' or 'lady')
thep angelic being
torasap telephone
tuk-tuk three-wheeled motor samlor

upekkhâ the quality of equanimity

Vassa (*phansa*) Buddhist 'Lent'

wai traditional greeting (palms pressed together as in prayer)
wan daytime
wang palace
wat temple
witthayu radio

yaa baa methamphetamine

Index

All You Want to Know About Thailand, from
ASIA BOOKS

The Thai and I:
Successful Living in Thailand
By Roger Welty

A must for anyone who lives in Thailand, especially first-time
visitors, expats, and businesspeople. This informative
guide sheds light on how to understand and adapt to Thai
culture—in order to get the most out of your life here.

**The second *Thai and I* book provides vital information on:
arriving and adjusting to your new home; family life and
pressures; working in Thailand; managing domestic help;
maintaining your mental health; living in Bangkok or
upcountry; getting around; and how to deal with goodbyes.**

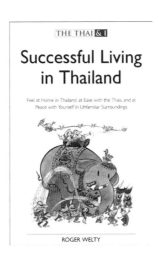

Bridging the Gap:
Managing the Cross-Cultural Workplace in Thailand
By Kriengsak Niratpattanasai

Bridging the Gap is a practical and entertaining guide to help foreign and Thai businesspeople working together in Thailand. The book is divided into four sections, starting with an insightful account of the Thai cultural make-up, and a revealing study on how Thais regard foreigners in the workplace, and vice versa. Real-life case studies highlight common misunderstandings and offer solutions for awkward situations. Also includes a section on how to handle official social functions such as weddings and funerals.

The Essential Guide for Anyone Who Works,
or Does Business, In Thailand

Managing the Cross-Cultural Workplace in Thailand

BRIDGING
THE
GAP

"Essential reading for anybody who wants to do business in Thailand.
It shall stand as a reference for future generations."
– Frank-Jurgen Richter, World Economic Forum.

KRIENGSAK NIRATPATTANASAI

Mai Pen Rai Means Never Mind
By Carol Hollinger

Carol Hollinger was a housewife, mother, and teacher, and *Mai Pen Rai* is her humorous, often hilarious account of her experience in all those roles during her stay in Thailand, where her husband was stationed in the US foreign service. A brilliant observer of customs, manners, and cultural differences, she writes frankly and unsparingly of herself and her fellow Americans, and relates both the fun and the frustration of communicating with Thai people—without being coy or condescending.

A Classic Book, Not Only For All Foreign Residents and Visitors, but Also for Thais Themselves.

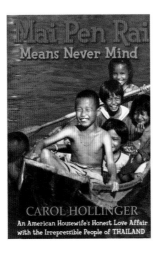

Learning Thai: Just Enough to Get By and More
By Warankna Tuwayanonde & Paul Wallis

A phrase book and guide for you to learn and understand Thai in a simple and comprehensive way. With this book you won't need a Thai teacher. When in doubt, just ask any Thai. Includes the necessary keys to the language, and examples of dialogue in Thai to help familiarize you with the Thai way of speaking.

Pronunciation. Grammar. Useful Words and Phrases for Travellers and Expats. Organized by Subject: (Shopping, Transport, Hotels, etc). Mini Dictionary.

**Bangkok People
By James Eckardt**

*"The killing starts around 8 p.m. and can go on till the
very early hours."* The pig butcher.

"Flying off to the Bahamas one day, Paris the next." The TV producer.

From business tycoons, bargirls, and bodysnatchers to street vendors,
slum-dwellers, socialites and singers, *Bangkok People* takes the reader
into the daily lives of city denizens—both Thai and expat, and from
the filthy rich to the just plain filthy. This fascinating, funny, sometimes serious and occasionally odd collection plunges right into the
heart of the myriad masses who make this mad metropolis tick.